Dave,
Great see
you in Denver –

Billy Miller

The NEW American Dream

Betty Miles

Pinpoint Press
Columbia, South Carolina

The New American Dream.

Published by Pinpoint Press,
A Belesprit Enterprise.

For information, write in care of Pinpoint Press, Post Office Box 5146, Columbia, South Carolina 29250.

ISBN 0-9648553-1-3

Library of Congress Cataloging-In-Publication Data available.

The NEW American Dream

Table of Contents

Introduction

This is a book for people who are ready to doubt.

We live in a cynical time, a time when people are ready to assume the worst, when the hardest thing to do is to believe in something, even ourselves.

As a lawyer and politician, I've felt the effects of this cynicism first hand. In 1990, during my first campaign for Secretary of State, I met an older woman on the streets of Marion, South Carolina, who told me: "I'm not voting for any incumbents or any lawyers." "Well, ma'am," I replied, "I'm not the incumbent, and I'm sure if you ask some of my clients, they'll tell you I'm not much of a lawyer, either."

When it comes to being "presumed guilty," the only industry with more PR problems than the law or politics would be network marketing. I see it when my wife—a very genuine, talented, competent and successful businesswoman—tells people she's in network marketing. They step back, glance nervously about and start mumbling about "pyramids." To be honest, that was my general impression of the industry, too.

I had seen too many chain letters and Ponzi schemes during my days as an attorney to put any credibility in the network marketing concept. So, when Betty first mentioned to me that she was looking at a network marketing business, without even thinking, I said "no."

But Betty, as you will see in the pages following, is no quitter. She kept working on me, challenging my assumptions. She scored points by noting that some people think all lawyers are shysters and all politicians are crooks, but we knew better, didn't we?

Finally, I agreed —unenthusiastically—to check it out.

After weeks of research, I concluded that my wife was absolutely right. Like most people, I knew nothing of the contemporary network marketing industry, about the changes in their business approach, the large, well-respected businesses that are using network marketing techniques every day. Indeed, my change of heart is so complete that not only have I concluded that network marketing that delivers a product or service at a competitive price is legal, but I truly believe it soon will represent the preferred method of delivery of products and services by major companies all over the world.

If you share the negative view of network marketing that I once had, this book is for you. It offers straight answers to your questions about how network marketing really works, about its legal status, its business structure and its compensation systems.

If you understand network marketing, but doubt that it is right for you, then you need this book as well. It tells the stories of people just like you—in their own words—and how they have changed their lives using network marketing to prosper in the new, down-sizing, high-pressure economy.

But most of all, this book is for those of you who have begun to doubt yourself, who have given up on the American Dream.

Like Betty, I am a dedicated believer in America as the land of opportunity. I am in politics because I want government to be more than a regulator and tax collector. I want government to be my partner—and yours—in achieving the American Dream of economic independence and personal freedom so you can live your life to the fullest—as decided by you, not someone else.

This is America. And in the America of the late 20th century, network marketing offers astounding rewards to those who dare to believe, who dare to dream and dare to achieve. This book will help you believe again by showing you that the dream is still alive. When you finish this book, whether or not you get involved in a single network marketing program, you will know that the bright vision of the future shared by our parents and grandparents is still alive; and, if you look, you might find the vision, too.

If you doubt me, then this book is for you.

Jim Miles
South Carolina Secretary of State
July 4, 1996

Tommy May God Bless You!

Preface

This book is a road map of my journey into network marketing and a snapshot of some of the special individuals I've been fortunate enough to cross paths with—and walk with a little way—on our journey to the top!

You will meet and touch the lives of a priest, a preacher, a minister, a missionary, a minister's wife, and many others who serve God every day.

You will hear about people with external handicaps such as blindness, deafness and the inability to walk. You will feel the pain, as well as experience the courage some of these people demonstrate as they suffer the debilitating effects of Lou Gehrig's Disease, Multiple Sclerosis, and other devastating illnesses. Their stories demonstrate that all of us have handicaps of one type or another—some people have theirs on the outside and some have emotional ones on the inside.

You will hear from a doctor, a dentist, a pharmacist, a teacher, a principal, a superintendent and a coach.

You will meet a lawyer, a detective, a politician, small company owners, large company owners, a real estate tycoon, a real estate franchise owner, a telephone company executive, insurance brokers and general agents, stock brokers and broker dealers. You will even hear from a former IRS agent who is happy and glad for you to be happy, too.

You will hear about many families—a young, disabled father with his wife and one year old son, a newlywed couple, a young couple planning their first child, and a father and mother who are both watching their daughter grow up.

You will hear about people making some part-time money so they don't have to "just get by" anymore, as well as people making enough to replace two family incomes.

You will hear about a young, 38-year-old basketball coach, who six years ago was earning $36,000 per year, and is now making a seven figure monthly income that is increasing rapidly.

You will hear about people giving up careers in such fields as law, teaching, coaching, medicine, real estate, insurance, and many others.

These people you will hear about range in age from 14 to 84.

Most of the people you will meet have never done network marketing before. What do all these people have in common? They believe in The New American Dream. They have taken control of their lives. They have hope and they are passing it on. We would love to share this hope with you.

I can never thank all of the people who helped make this book possible, but I want to mention a few who went out of their way to give me their support, both physically and emotionally. Many of them have paid a price and I am very grateful for their assistance.

First, I want to thank my husband, Jim, not only for his support during the grueling ordeal of writing a book, but especially for his support in my decision to do network marketing. Because of my schedule, he has been forced to make many banana sandwiches when he would have preferred a hot, home-cooked meal. And he went to bed alone many nights only to be rudely awakened when I stumbled into bed at 3:00 or 4:00 a.m. I have heard people say that menopause will not kill a wife, but it comes close to killing her husband. So does writing a book!

My children have also suffered without complaining, but they believe in this business, too, because they see how much it is doing for our family.

My precious mother, who is much of my inspiration and almost totally responsible for my positive outlook on life, has been greatly neglected. She only lives two hours away, but it might as well have been a thousand these last few months. Jim and I even missed joining her on a trip to Bermuda because of this book. Growing up, she was always there for me, no matter how much work she had to do. But instead of making me feel guilty during these trying times, she has just loved me and let me know that she understands. She also helped me proof some of the book and we both cried together over the chapter about Daddy. We miss him a lot.

I appreciate Trudy Wilson, my husband's sister, who has helped me as an assistant, but more importantly, has encouraged me and had confidence in me every step of the way.

I want to thank Catherine Bennett, my administrative assistant, for putting up with all of the confusion, the messy stacks of paper she found every morning after she sorted and left everything perfectly organized the afternoon before, for her patience during our long typing sessions when she typed while I talked and changed my mind and talked some more, and changed my mind and talked some more. She is truly a special person.

I am also grateful to Dana Woodrum for her tireless efforts in editing and proofing before she left for Europe. Her sunny personality and cheerful attitude always made me feel better after a long sleepless night of writing.

Thanks to Jennifer Graham for the final proofing. I'm sure her professional expertise has enhanced this book significantly. She is a very gifted and creative writer.

Many people have contributed to this book; some through interviews, some through written accounts of their networking experience. These individuals were selected because they each have contributed something special to this industry, and they exemplify the adventurous, entrepreneurial spirit and stubborn tenacity that is making network marketing a credible, exciting, extraordinary method for marketing products and services. The editors could not use all of the stories, and they had a great deal of difficulty choosing. But I want to give my heartfelt thanks to each of the following for their inspiration as well as their friendship.

Ralph and Karen Golson, who closed down an insurance business to do network marketing full time; Dick and Nancy Powlas, who look forward to closing down several small businesses; George Curry, a former IBM executive, and his daughter, Marsha; Scottie and Lori Salter and their little son, Jake; Gary and Alice Weathersby, who love this business because it gives them more time to fish and hunt;

Rochelle Middleton, who lost her husband and is using this business to send her kids to college; Ken and Betty Lou Perkins; Vern Hawkins; Dr. Ann Myers; Carol Johnson and Joanne Jones, my superstars in Statesville, North Carolina; Bob and Margaret Johnson who love to work this business together;

Darla Stahl, a dynamic insurance lady; Bill and Heather Wells, a young newlywed couple who plan to do network marketing full-time from the very beginning of their lives together; Kenny Gilmore, one of the most dedicated and genuine leaders in our business; and Kathy LaVallee, a precious friend, who plans to use her income to help her minister husband and many missionaries around the world.

And last, but not least, my editor and very dear friend, Michael Graham, who has literally pulled every word of this book right out of me. He has been unbelievably patient with a first-time writer, and he is a terrific motivator. I love you all.

And, of course, I want to thank you, for giving me this opportunity to share my experiences with you. I truly believe that the stories you will read in this book will change your life, just as they have changed mine.

– Betty Miles

chapter one

What Happened to the American Dream?

For my father, it began by running away from home and joining the Merchant Marines. For one son, it meant going to Baylor and studying to become a minister; for another, it meant facing the furor of The Citadel—The Military College of South Carolina.

And for me? It began with marriage and ended in divorce. It began as a housewife and ended near bankruptcy and $300,000 in debt.

It's the American Dream.

All my life, I've been chasing that dream, the dream of financial prosperity, personal happiness and a safe, secure retirement. And as a young girl, growing up in Charleston, South Carolina, it seemed as certain as the coming dawn.

I grew up in an average, all-American town, part of an average, all-American family believing, like most of the kids around me, that I was entitled to—and would one day be able to live—the "American Dream"! I was the oldest of five children—three sisters and a brother—and we all felt the same. We were positive we would all experience the American Dream because our parents taught us that it was ours to achieve. All it would take is hard work, a good education, a little tenacity, and we would be on our way.

But something has changed in the past 30 years.

For millions of us, the dream of financial freedom and security is nothing more than a dream.

For example, in 1995 alone, more than 500,000 American workers lost their jobs. In the month of January, 1996, 100,000 more working Americans joined them.

The American Dream—it's a phrase thrown around at every political rally, press conference and public school assembly. But what does it mean?

I asked my friends and family. It is a little bit different for everyone, but eventually it comes down to this: Living the American Dream means working hard at everything you do, getting a good education, finding a good job, and raising a family. It also means enjoying the fruits of your efforts—owning your own home, living well, retiring comfortably, and watching your children discover the dream for themselves. The American Dream is the confident hope in our country and in ourselves.

This is what I believe, which is why I was so saddened to hear a CNN report recently that 62% of Americans no longer believe they can achieve the American Dream. This is not just bad news—it is a crisis! For losing hope in the Dream means we are losing hope in ourselves and in our nation.

Well, I am not ready to lose hope. I know the American Dream still lives, because I have found it. Thousands of people like you and me have discovered that, though the pathways have changed, The American Dream of our parents and grandparents can still be achieved.

We don't need to lose our dreams; we only need to open our eyes to a new way of finding the economic freedom and security we desire.

However, while we can still reach the American Dream, we must honestly acknowledge that more and more Americans are struggling and falling short. White collar professionals, blue collar workers, corporate managers, 4.0 college graduates—all are working harder than ever, but few are actually moving closer to achieving financial independence and security.

Why? Let's look at the American Dream and the economic realities that are reshaping it in the 1990s. Once again, I am defining the American Dream as our heartfelt belief that *if we work hard and get a good education, we will find a good job that will allow us to own a home, raise a family, and retire in comfort.*

"Work hard..."

If hard work alone were enough to achieve the American Dream, my father would have been President of the United States.

The Fili household personified the Protestant work ethic, both demonstrated and enforced by my father and mother, Frank and Florrie Fili. Dad grew up rapidly in Philadelphia. His mother died when he was only eight years old. When his father remarried a few years later, Dad didn't get along with his stepmother, so at the age of 15 he ran away and joined the Merchant Marines. He had to lie about his age, but he got in and never went home again.

From the Merchant Marines he went to the Navy where he spent the next 21 years and retired before he had even turned 40! A lifetime of work behind him, he didn't relax. Instead, he started a new career...as an accountant.

As a 15-year-old Merchant Marine, my father obviously had not finished high school.

However, he used the opportunities presented by the Navy to get his high school equivalency and eventually earn a BS degree in accounting. After the Navy, he took a civil service position with the Air Force and worked nights as an accountant for Thomas and Howard, a large wholesale food company. For my dad, retirement meant going from one job to two!

My mother also had a terrific work ethic and was just as determined that her children's lives would be easier than her own. Her family was poor because her father died in his early forties, leaving her mother alone to provide for six children. My grandmother worked at various odd jobs, from babysitting to selling Avon, but she never gave up. She managed to keep her six children together, and my mother said they never felt poor because they were so happy. Mother met and married my dad in Georgia when she was only 20 years old.

For as long as I can remember, Mother was always figuring out ways to bring in additional income for the family. She ran a day-care center in our home and sometimes there were as many as 10 children living in our small, three-bedroom home. But it never felt crowded—we loved the kids, and the only problem I can remember is all those kids fighting over one bathroom! Some of the children were there only during the day while their mothers were working, but others were there for weeks at a time, day and night.

Mother and Dad were always working and their primary goal in life—particularly for my father—was to send all five of their children to college. That was Dad's American Dream for us. He was determined to give my siblings and me the opportunity to live the good life, to avoid the hard work he had been forced to do all his life. He never begrudged working hard to help us, but he absolutely didn't want us to have the same kind of life.

That was his "contract" with America: I'll work hard, send my kids to college, and if I do, the American economy will make room for them and provide a career at a big corporation somewhere with lots of benefits and a lifetime of security.

Dad lived just long enough to keep his end of the bargain. He saw all five children graduate from prestigious American universities. Soon thereafter, he passed away, and I know he was a happy man.

However, he would have been saddened to see how difficult it has become to find any real security in our society. If he had lived, it would have distressed him to know that his grandchildren were graduating from college without the prospect of a job. He lived his entire life without hearing the words "downsizing" or "forced retirements." He couldn't have imagined millions of white collar workers being laid off by America's blue chip corporations.

But if you're an experienced middle manager suddenly looking for a job, or an ambitious hourly employee who has seen real wages remain flat while your company's profits have risen sharply, you have come to realize, as Frank Fili's children and grandchildren did, that hard work is no longer a sure ticket to the American Dream.

"...get a good education..."

My husband and I have five sons—four of them between the ages of 23 and 28. Between 1989 and 1995, each one of them graduated from a prominent university, all with good grades. And not one of them received a single corporate job offer. Not one.

The same is true for their wives and girlfriends—all over-achievers in college, but not recruited as graduates.

This is a drastic change from my college days when IBM and other large corporations would set up booths at the University of South Carolina hoping to lure graduates with incentives like company cars, big expense accounts and country club memberships. Not any more! Today, instead of offering incentives to attract new employees, they offer early retirement incentives to old ones!

It's difficult not to feel sorry for this year's college graduates—and the parents who paid their bills. It has always been true that a college degree meant a 10-40% increase in lifetime earnings when compared to a high school diploma, and this gap is widening. However, what is not commonly reported is that a large factor is a decline in real wages for low skill workers—NOT a surge in income for college grads.

Yes, it is also true that college degrees in specialty fields—computers, biotechnology, etc.—are still prized, but if you don't happen to be the next Bill Gates, this trend is not very comforting. The bottom line is this: For intelligent, well-rounded college grads, the sheepskin is no longer a moneybag.

Some young people are trying to overcome this trend by getting even more education. The number of master's degrees awarded in the 1990s is 53% higher than in the 1970s. And American universities, which graduated a total of 30,000 Ph.D.s in 1970, generated a whopping 42,000 doctoral degrees in 1995.

The result is simple economics: The more you have of something, the less it is worth. The value of a doctorate—once a prized possession—has declined from oversupply. Professional resumes are now filled with "post-doctoral" study references to raise the applicant's stature.

Meanwhile, a bachelor's degree—once the mantra of the American Dream—is almost as common as a high school ring. The inherent value of the diploma has all but disappeared.

The effect of this trend is terrible for our young people, many of whom leave college with tens of thousands of dollars in student loans, but a degree worth only a fraction of that amount. A young lady recently graduated from the University of South Carolina with a student loan debt of more than $50,000! She had switched majors many times and ended up with a degree in archeology, a degree she had no intention of ever using.

One of the student aid workers told me: "We're supposed to be doing these kids a favor by giving them loans, but they end up $50,000 in the hole and have nothing to show for it. If we had just bought her a house with that money, she would at least have a place to sleep while she's unemployed."

College educations are wonderful things to have and wonderful experiences for our children. The point I want to make, however, is that the days when a college degree guaranteed a good-paying job—or meant the beginning of a successful career—are long gone. It takes something more.

"...find a good job..."

Believe me, I have had some GREAT jobs in my lifetime. The problem word in that sentence is "had."

When Henry Ford and the other barons of America's young

industrial age began the Corporate Era, they introduced a relatively new possibility for American workers: Learn one job, learn it well, work for one employer your entire life, and retire. Before the Corporate Era, the only lifetime employment was on the farm, or maybe as a business owner yourself. It was common for tradesmen to travel from job to job, and workers could expect a lifetime of seeking work.

The notion of "lifetime employment" didn't catch on until the early 20th century. Then, the unionization of America after World War II solidified it, and the economic boom of the 1950s and 60s made it part of our economic vision for ourselves and our children.

But, while no one was watching, the economy changed. We can expect approximately seven or more job changes in our working lifetimes. Jobs with large corporations are disappearing, while job growth among smaller companies (100 employees or fewer) has exploded. Since 1992, four out of five new jobs were created by businesses with fewer then 50 employees.

Meanwhile, corporate downsizing has limited the number of salaried, white collar jobs available. And the employees who remain are keenly aware that the job they count on today may be gone tomorrow.

I recently saw a chilling cartoon in the newspaper featuring a politician at an after-dinner speech announcing "This administration has created 7.8 million jobs!" Behind him is the waiter, thinking "Yeah, and I have THREE of them!"

The very definition of what makes a good job—a high salary, lots of benefits, job security, etc.—is beginning to change. More and more of us are making compromises, scaling back our own American dream. "Well, working for the government doesn't pay as much," one young woman told me recently, "but I need the health care." Or another who said: "I like the salary, but they can't guarantee that I'll have a job this time next year."

The result is that finding a "good" job is harder then ever—if not impossible.

For example, one of our "college-graduate" sons went to work for an office machinery company. He's bright, hard-working and a good salesman. Within the first three months, he earned more than $50,000. Of course, he had to call on thirty businesses a day to get those results, but he did it.

However, instead of encouraging him, the company quickly offered him a position in management with an annual income in the twenties, making sure he understood his future advancement depended on his contributions as a manager. In other words, taking this pay cut was the only way he could continue his journey up the corporate ladder. They did explain that he would make a small percentage of commission on the sales of the reps he hired and trained. I'm sure large companies hope that a gifted salesman will be able to teach many others to sell successfully, but that is not the way it usually works.

The current corporate climate, particularly in this era of high dividends and immediate profitability, makes it harder for "good" employees to succeed at "good" jobs. The Peter Principle pushes high performers up the ladder into management, instead of leaving them in the sales force where they can excel.

In the end, it may be that the only "good" jobs left in America are the ones we create ourselves.

" ... and retire comfortably!"

If you are a baby boomer, you've got a lot to worry about. In 1996, the first "official" baby boomers began turning 50, and teen-agers who grew up with long hair and The Beatles, are moving on to Grecian Formula and Geritol.

And what happens when we turn 65? According to a new book by Robert Samuelson, if we are to have the same retirement benefits as our parents, our children will have to pay 50% more in taxes...on top of what they must also pay for our $5 trillion national debt.

Will our children and grandchildren be willing to do this? Or will the benefits available at retirement be scaled back? The only certainty is that it will be harder than ever to retire in comfort in the 21st century.

And there is more bad news for those of us planning a future of fishin' and free time. The corporate downsizing of the 1980s and 1990s has decreased the number of American workers with employer-funded pensions. Former middle managers who counted on large companies like IBM or AT&T for their retirement are now out on their own, and are more likely to depend on our government's retirement benefits when they reach 65.

With Social Security and Medicare on the verge of bankruptcy, many Americans are struggling to survive after they reach the age of retirement.

With approximately 12 percent of Americans over 65 living in poverty in the 1990s, imagine what is going to happen when the Baby Boomers start to retire!

Many people have the idea that you turn 65, you stop working, and you live the high life in Hilton Head or West Palm Beach. But those of us thinking about our financial futures know that it is not that simple. Nobody is going to hand us an easy retirement, and for many of us, the question is whether we will ever be able to afford to retire.

For our financial futures to be secure, we must act now. If we rely on the government, we may be in serious trouble when we try to enjoy our "golden years."

Politicians are always talking about less government, and the American people seem to agree. But less government will mean less benefits for us as taxpayers. And with retirees becoming a larger and larger portion of the population, something is bound to change. If we establish our own retirement savings, we can be assured that we will have the financial security to enjoy our retirement.

That is why we must seize the financial opportunities given to us now.

You can achieve the American Dream!

The American dream was what I pursued in the 1950s, began to live in the 1960s, chased tirelessly through the 1970s, seemed to lose in the 1980s. That was the bad news.

This book is about the good news.

This book tells the story of dozens of people just like you, people who found a new way to realize their dream of financial independence and security. They discovered, as I have, that the dream isn't dead at all. It is alive and well, and thousands of people are finding it every day.

They are finding a new path to personal wealth and prosperity—not climbing the old corporate ladder, but riding a new wave of business opportunity called "network marketing."

Network marketing is to the next century what franchising was to this one: A revolutionary change in the way America does business; an economic revolution that is bringing prosperity to a new generation of hard-working men and women.

There is nothing magic about network marketing. It still takes hard work, intelligence and tenacity to succeed. But unlike the cumbersome corporate-marketplace, there are no layoffs or downsizing. You create your own opportunity, you develop your own markets, and you control your own destiny.

With network marketing, your achievements are only limited by your imagination.

If you are skeptical, or if you have questions about the business concepts of network marketing, read on. In these pages, you will hear first-hand from the achievers, from people who once felt their chance to achieve the American Dream was lost.

Today, they have achieved financial independence and prosperity beyond their wildest dreams. And you can, too.

Read on...

real-life stories

Beth Hinson

Beth Hinson is a sparkling firecracker of a lady, full of energy, ability, and determination. I remember the first time I saw her.

I was doing a business presentation at the Omni Hotel in Charleston, South Carolina, two years ago. I noticed a petite, young woman staring intently at me, as if she were hypnotized.

After the meeting, she rushed up to me and introduced herself and her son, who looked more like her younger brother. The name Beth Hinson didn't ring any bells with me at the time, but I knew she was special. I could sense the power exuding from her. A few weeks later, she tracked me down in Columbia and we made an appointment for her to attend one of my training classes.

After a few short moments with Beth, I knew she was going to be a shining star in network marketing. She had the tenacity and the talent to roar right to the top, and that's exactly what she did. Today, Beth is one of the highest paid females in the country, and she's just getting started. Her greatest attribute, however, is not her ability to create income for herself; it's her ability to make ordinary people feel that they can do it, too.

"When I was approached about network marketing, I thought I was too busy for it," says Beth, mother of two. "I was too busy going broke as a real estate broker."

Like many people from small town America, she waited tables and worked on a farm. She discovered she was a born salesman completely by accident. Working in the cucumber shed of a commercial farm, she discovered some fire extinguishers the farmer had tried to sell but had given up on.

"I asked him if I could try," says Beth. "So I'd take these fire extinguishers into a businessman's office, place a briefcase on the desk, squirt it with lighter fluid and set it on fire!

That got their attention. Then, I'd use the fancy fire extinguisher to put it out—they were a special kind that didn't make a mess—and I'd sell to EVERYONE!"

That's the kind of lady Beth is. She really knows how to make an impression!

"I made $800 in one week selling these odd little fire extinguishers, and I thought 'I have never seen this much money before in my life!' Then one day the fire marshal marched into my office with a cease-and-desist order. These fire extinguishers weren't UL approved! I was breaking the law! Here I was, a single mom with two small children and the first time in my life I had made some real money, they were going to lock me up for it."

But Beth is no quitter. She went on to get her real estate license and eventually started her own brokerage company. She had some successes, but there were challenges, too.

"Real estate sales are complicated. You've got rules and regulations, licenses and liens, lead in the paint and lawyers all around. It was like pulling teeth—and that's AFTER you had sold the customer. I was working too hard for too little money."

Beth's son introduced her to

a long-distance network marketing company, but she wasn't interested. "I thought of network marketing as a cultish thing," says Beth. "I'd see people get involved in it, treat it almost like a religion and never make any money. But my son was very insistent, so I called Betty Miles and she told me I should at least go to a meeting and listen."

In Beth's case, as in so many others, it was her relationship with someone close—her son—who convinced her to open up to the opportunity of network marketing.

"As we pulled into the parking lot, I noticed it was filled with Mercedes and Jaguars. My father always told me, 'If you want to be a winner, do what the winners are doing.' In the room that night was the largest independent real estate broker in my state. After the meeting, he turned to me and said, 'Beth, we're in the wrong business.'

And I said, 'Bob, I'm getting out of the wrong business.'

"So I went back to the my brokerage company and said 'I'm leaving'. They said, 'You can't leave, you own the company.' And I said, 'Watch me!' "

Today, Beth Hinson is extremely successful in network marketing. "To me, network marketing isn't anything strange or magical. It's just believing in yourself and the people you know. It's helping others find the greatness in themselves. If you expect the best and you profess the best, you're going to get it."

And Beth is a living example of someone who does just that. She understands what a wonderful opportunity network marketing can be for everyone. You don't need a college degree, a lot of money or a dog-eat-dog attitude.

"I love network marketing because you can't make money unless you're willing to help other people make money, too. When you start network marketing, no one asks you for a credit rating, employment record, not even a prison record. All you need is spirit and integrity," Beth says.

Beth's financial goal is $100,000 of monthly income by the end of the year, and she's right on target.

real-life stories

Paul Orberson

Paul Orberson, another high achiever, had almost given up on the American Dream. He started out in network marketing with a goal of $1,000 per month. Five and a half years later, he had added three zeros to that monthly income.

Paul Orberson is a legend. At the time of this writing, he was, according to *Upline Magazine,* earning in excess of $1 million a month in network marketing!

What does a $12 million dollar (and growing) annual income mean to a former high school basketball coach?

"All money means is freedom," says Paul. "And I want to be real free."

In 1990, Paul was a high school basketball coach in Boyle County, KY, teaching school and building a home for his family. A friend of his was involved in network marketing, but—believe it or not—one of America's most successful network marketers didn't find the idea appealing.

"My attitude was like a lot of people. I thought it was

something for other people but not for me. I thought, 'Hey, I went to college, I don't need this. Network marketing is for desperate people who couldn't find nothin' else to do and no one else to give 'em a job.' "

In fact, Paul's father was involved in A.L. Williams, a network marketing company that provided financial services. Paul went to several meetings but never got involved.

"I figured I was still too young, that I hadn't had time to get beat up by the world yet," confesses Paul. "Some of us have got to get beat up a little bit to appreciate an opportunity."

"When I finally went to a presentation, I guess I was ready. I was perfect for network marketing, because I didn't have a big-time life going; I didn't have to go to the country club and explain what I was doing. I was raising a family, coaching ball and going broke."

"A friend took me to my first presentation, and to be honest, I didn't know too much, but I signed up because I trusted my friend. That still happens in network marketing every day.

"People get involved to help their friends, and end up helping themselves, too."

Paul is so amazingly successful because he really does want to help people.

"All network marketing is," says Paul, "is getting yourself started in a business where you help other people, and by doing that, you make money. Selfish people get weeded out real quick, because you can't get paid unless you help someone else get paid. There is something inherently right about that."

Paul's success didn't come by accident. He worked hard, and he did an excellent job of reaching his network of connections in coaching. He would sometimes travel hundreds of miles just to meet with a single prospect. As a result, high school and college coaches from across Kentucky, Indiana and Ohio got involved in his downline.

"That's basically who my core business was built with—not business people, not fancy people," says Orberson. "From day one, I worked my butt off. Today, I'm still working to help those people I got started in this business, because I told them that it would work for them."

"This business is no good if I'm the only person who can make money," says Paul.

What kind of people tend to succeed in network marketing?

"I am living proof that anybody, ANYBODY can make this business work," laughs Paul, who claims a modest IQ of 92. "But you have to be motivated. When I got started in this business, I was eaten up with making something of myself. I had finally gotten to the point in my life where I decided it would be okay for me to get rich."

"One key to success in network marketing is credibility with the people you're talking to.

That's most of the battle. They have to know you understand and believe in what you're doing."

Paul also adds: "People who do well in this business don't use logic. People who do well are emotional, they are excited about their chance to do well, to achieve their dreams. Logic is not emotional, it has no energy. It takes a passion and energy."

Does Paul believe that the American Dream is dead? Absolutely not!

"You hear people sayin' that it takes hard work, dedication, passion and training to succeed.

"But look at the Alamo. They were certainly prepared, passionate and well-trained. Every day people are getting slaughtered in business, playing by rules that don't work.

"One problem," Paul explains, "is that it's hard to find people to teach you how to get rich.

"Teachers are all broke, so they can't help. And the people who know how are usually too busy making money to tell you how to do it. Network marketing on the other hand, pays successful people for teaching YOU how to succeed, and the more they succeed, the more money you make. It's pretty simple."

And Paul is the perfect example, still working hard to help his downline (and his bottom line) grow.

"People need to realize that, in network marketing, you're building a business, you're building equity. That's what most of us don't have in our jobs. Think about it: You can sell your network just like a business owner selling a restaurant or an auto parts store. It's a business.

"And here's the neat little part. In network marketing, you get paid for what you START, not for what you DO. In most jobs, you only get paid for what you do that day. Today, I've been sitting by the pool. If I got paid for what I did today, I'd be broke. But because of what I started, a network of 60,000 or more long distance customer gatherers, I'm getting paid today. And tomorrow and the next day.

"Getting paid for what you do doesn't work," Paul says flatly.

"You need to get paid for what you start."

These two superstars exemplify what this book is all about. Ordinary people who have become extraordinary! Beth Hinson and Paul Orberson have achieved financial independence and prosperity beyond their wildest dreams. And you can, too.

Read about more extraordinary people at the end of the following chapters.

chapter two

How I Found the New American Dream

(And you can, too!)

I was listening to Rush Limbaugh on the radio not long ago, and I heard a woman calling from New Jersey. She was clearly frustrated, angry and hurting.

"My husband and I are in our forties," she explained, "and we have done everything we were supposed to do to be successful in America. We went to college, got good jobs and worked hard to take care of our family.

"My husband worked his way up the corporate ladder for 20 years and made his company a lot of money," she went on, her frustration blaring from my car radio. "And now, after being promoted to one of the highest positions in the company, they suddenly decided they didn't need him anymore. So, right before Christmas and with no warning, he was laid off."

"That was a year ago," she continued. "This year, I was laid off by the company I've been working for since our children started school. It's time for our kids to go to college, and my husband and I are back at square one."

She described herself as part of the "newly ignored" generation, the middle-aged, middle-class, middle management people who have been playing by the economic rules for 20 years, only to discover that the game has changed.

As I listened to this woman share her fear and frustration, I knew I was hearing the voice of thousands of Americans—middle class people who grew up believing that their financial destiny was set, only to discover years later that the changing economy of the 1990s brought an uncertain future. Fifty-one percent of Americans worry about their own jobs when they hear of companies downsizing and laying off employees.

What do you do when you lose your job after a lifetime in a corporate bureaucracy? What do you do when the economic tide washes away the small business you've invested your life in?

What happens to workers who see the only trade they've ever known wiped out by new technology or foreign competition?

You change; you learn; you adapt. You believe in yourself and look for a new way to achieve the personal and financial success you desire. If the traditional doors to economic opportunity are closing, don't get frustrated and beat your head against them. Instead, open a new door!

It's been said that a sure sign of insanity is doing the same things the same way, but expecting a different result. It may not be insane, but it sure can be frustrating. I know, because I've tried all the usual pathways to success—owning a business, commissioned sales, even working in a traditional bureaucracy. But I never achieved, or had the hope of achieving, the financial independence and growing income that I dreamed of. I just worked twice as hard in the same old ways, and became twice as frustrated.

Then, I discovered the new way.

How I found Network Marketing

On paper, Betty Miles is the most UNLIKELY candidate for network marketing in the world.

First of all, I wasn't desperate. According to the stereotypes, network marketing is only for people who have failed at everything. While it's true that some people have used network marketing to lift themselves up from poverty, when I started my network marketing career, I was making more than $100,000 a year with my own insurance business.

Secondly, I'm not what people call a network marketing "junkie." There is a handful of people who spend their lives jumping from program to program, waiting for lightning to strike. I know now that you can make your own lightning with the power of network marketing. But when I was first approached, I wasn't thinking that way at all.

In fact, I had been involved in a failed network marketing scheme years ago. I was what they call "once bitten, twice shy." But at the same time, I was ready for a change.

Traditional business owners will tell you that while success is possible, the amount of work involved is enormous. And the problem with traditional businesses is that the work never ends. You work like a dog until—if you're lucky—someone buys you out. But for most small businesses, that day never comes. We spend our lives working to build the business, maintain a modest income and retire broke. That's the path I was on when my neighbors told me about network marketing.

In 1993, my husband Jim and I were lucky enough to have Steve and Kathy Newton for next-door neighbors. Steve was the head basketball coach at the University of South Carolina, and Kathy was a science teacher. We had really enjoyed getting to know them. We both had boys about the same age and Jim and Steve walked together every evening. While they were walking they would talk about going into business together one day (they both had the entrepreneurial spirit). We heard about many different ventures they were considering, from buying a car wash to opening a pizza parlor.

Three years ago, Steve went to a coaches' meeting in Kentucky and came back talking about some new telecommunications business. Since Jim had been discussing other business opportunities with Steve he was receptive when Steve suggested that it would be great for me to work this business with Kathy.

Kathy was one of my closest friends so I was interested in

finding a business that we could do together. They brought a video to our home that evening, and as soon as we realized it was network marketing, Jim glared at me and shook his head, making it perfectly clear that he was not pleased with even the possibility of my getting involved.

But what I saw that night really got the wheels in my head spinning. I knew the life insurance industry was making drastic changes. Many companies were selling policies directly to the public, bypassing the agents, via television ads and the Internet. All of which meant I would soon be working harder, and probably for less money.

It was a miracle that I even looked at the network marketing opportunity with Steve and Kathy that day, but when I saw that video about a national long distance company that was offering people the opportunity to start an independent business which required no inventory, no deliveries to make, no money to collect from the customers, no quotas and no complicated math or paperwork, I said, "YES!"

The combination of telecommunications with network marketing was the proverbial light at the end of the tunnel. After fully investigating the company with my husband, I signed right up. I felt this was the way I would use my talents, find financial security, and be a success!

I couldn't wait to start! Since this business was relatively new to our state, there was no one to train me or Kathy. We floundered around and did many things wrong, but our enthusiasm was contagious and spread like a virus. And I absolutely loved every minute of it.

This is the key to network marketing: You are selling success. Sure, some of your customers are only that—customers. You are a business person providing a product or service. But the way to make big money in network marketing is to create more network marketers and put them in your downline. Then these people gather their own customers, and you get paid for them, too!

And the more I shared this business with other people, the more I saw it change their lives. That's a very motivating experience—helping others find hope, to help them provide for their families, to help them build a secure financial future for themselves and their children.

In network marketing, my special gift of selling fits perfectly. I discovered that I was not only a closer, but a motivator! I was able to convince people that they could succeed, too. I think I convinced them because I truly believed it myself. I honestly believed anyone—regardless of age, sex, race or education—could make network marketing work if they were willing to pay the price.

And what is that price?

You have to be willing to do the things unsuccessful people refuse to do.

I'm willing to pay the price because, for those of us who just keep trying one more day and never quit, the rewards are so great: not just financially, but emotionally and spiritually as well. I am so grateful to the Newtons for helping me see the bright future ahead. And even though it is a lot of work, sharing this incredible opportunity with thousands of people is my purpose in life. As I have said before, we all need to decide what our true purpose is and mine is helping people find hope. There is no better vehicle for that purpose.

Now, before you get the idea that I was born to do network marketing, let me tell you that I spent my first nine months in the business as a coward! I wouldn't shut down my brokerage company, and I only worked the network business part time. In that short time, my income reached the same level as my renewal income. I was so surprised that I decided to split my time 50/50 between my "real" job (the brokerage) and my network business. At nine months, my monthly income had reached $17,000, and I knew that I had to go full-time. My income has continued to grow as has my respect for this industry and the unbelievable power of network marketing.

Network marketing is so much fun that at one point I actually began to resent the time I spent selling life insurance. Who wants to sell a product people have to die to get? With my network business, I love getting up in the morning, and I'm excited about my work.

I often think of one of my favorite quotations, "Life is an exciting adventure, or it is nothing." Do you know who said that? Helen Keller! She was born blind, deaf and mute. But even she could see that the joy of life is in the adventure.

And network marketing is kind of like the Navy: "It's not just a job, it's an adventure!"

The adventure comes for your pursuit of limitless success. And I mean that literally—"limitless." There are people in network marketing who are actually earning hundreds of thousands every month!

I know of one marketer who has a million dollar monthly income which is growing steadily. They are people just like you, people who have seen the opportunity and have seized it for themselves.

Once again, to be successful, you have to be willing to do the things that unsuccessful people refuse to do. If you are willing to do those things—work hard, care about others and motivate them to join you on this new path—you can achieve wealth and prosperity you never imagined!

real-life stories

Mack Ballard

Mack Ballard used to be a tough, Clint Eastwood type of detective, dealing with murderers and thugs and all sorts of criminal elements, but God brought him to his knees, and now he's a gentle, loving man with a passion for helping others. It's truly amazing. He told me he rarely ever asks people to come into his network marketing business because God just sends them to him. I asked Mack why he considered network marketing, and this is what he told me:

"A friend of mine from Columbia, South Carolina called me a year and a half ago and told me about a telecommunications company looking for marketers. He said I could do it part-time. I felt negative about it, and I fought for a couple of weeks because I didn't want to do anything outside the ministry. I've been in the ministry full time for 12 years and it has been my sustenance, but we had come to take over a mission church and a small Christian school, so there wasn't much money for us. We kept hitting our savings and it was getting frustrating, so I started praying, 'O God, please send me something. I need some help here financially.' Along came this friend with the network marketing deal, and it wasn't in a package that I wanted, so I rejected it. I told my little sister, Pam, and she said, 'You just need to pray about it.' I prayed about it: 'O God, help me. If I could just make $1000 a month extra doing something.'

"Sometimes opportunities come in packages that we don't understand—that are not normal, certainly not normal compared to what I was used to. I had grown up real poor in a mill village family. Our rent was $20 a month, with no bathtub. If you made a $100 a week when I was a kid, we thought you were rich, so this telecommunications thing was way over my head. My little sister called me back and said, 'You've been praying for help for your finances and you know that story you told about the guy who, during a flood, was on his front porch praying to God to get him out of it. Two boats and a helicopter came by as the water was rising and offered to take him to safety, but Bill told each of them that God was going to take care of him. After he drowned and went to heaven, he asked God, 'What happened?' God said, 'Bill, you dummy, I sent two boats and a helicopter.' My little sister said, 'Mac, I believe the Lord showed me that this is your helicopter and you need to do it.'

"That's when I knew in my heart I was supposed to do this network marketing thing, but I wasn't sure I could do it. I didn't want it to get me out of the ministry. I finally decided to try it, and my friend came down and put me in.

"I made a little money and got a little excited, but I was still praying 'God, just let me make $1000 a month.' My mind couldn't stretch to expect more, but the second month I made over a $1000. It was exciting. I worked a little bit and then for a while I didn't do anything. We had a death in our family and a lot of hard things and my counseling load was real heavy at the church. I just really laid it down for almost six months, and these little checks kept coming. I couldn't believe it.

"I picked it back up and started working it a little bit part-time. I was averaging six to ten hours a week, and the ministry was still going good. I started making a little money and helping the Christian school. We were able to buy six computers for the school because of this part-time business. We also paid cash for two Pentiums for the church office.

"Probably the reason I'm still doing this part-time business is because I'm a dreamer. The strongest dream in my life is to have a successful ministry and that takes finances. We want to build a "sheep shed." That's what we call a church here. We want it to be a multi-purpose building. This part-time money has really helped our building fund. We're looking for land now for the church, and it looks like we're going to have this dream come true.

"Also, I've had a personal dream all of my life. I wanted to live on a lake. We have a large lake around Milledgeville, Georgia called Lake Sinclair. Here I am, at 41, about to experience that dream. A few months ago we closed on our lake lot, and soon we will begin building, so I'm experiencing that dream.

"This thing really does work, and it teaches you one thing for sure: When you make enough people successful, you will realize success yourself. This is a wonderful business."

Mack Ballard is an inspiration to all who know him. He has influenced many ministers to come into this business, as well as prominent professionals, and people from all walks of life.

He is an expert on human nature and he teaches a course he calls "Fathering your downline."

It is a relationship study on how to treat people, how to motivate people, how to love people, and most of all, how to help people. He has pure motives and because of this, his business is flourishing.

real-life stories

John & Beth Craver

John and Beth Craver are two of my heroes in the network marketing industry. Not long ago, they found out that John had a devastating, fatal disease for which there is no cure. This beautiful young couple is an inspiration to all who know and love them, and I want to share their positive message with you. Beth had these comments when I asked her how they became involved in network marketing.

"John and I owned and operated our own video photography agency for eight years. We did weddings, conventions, and other special events, and were successful in our business; but we had goals and dreams we couldn't attain through the video business alone. One can only do so many weddings on a weekend. We wanted more, but didn't want to give up the freedom of remaining entrepreneurs. We were always looking for ways to subsidize our income.

"A year ago we were approached about a telecommunication networking opportunity. John and I knew the power of this industry through our video magazines, so before we even heard the company plan, we knew we were going to do it. It was so exciting to be a part of such an explosive industry and we enthusiastically began to share it with everyone we knew. This was the vehicle we needed to reach our goals.

"We had been actively working our new business for approximately six months when John was diagnosed with Lou Gehrig's disease; a debilitating and progressive disease of the muscles with no treatment or cure. It was so unexpected, so devastating! The new business was going so well that we had just decided to sell our video company so we could do the network marketing full-time. Ironically, we would have had to sell anyway because the progression of the disease made it impossible for John to do the video work. He no longer had total use of his hands and had slurring of speech.

"Believe it or not, it was one of the happiest day of our lives when we sold that business.

"Network marketing has given us the hope we needed to survive. We are so grateful to our upline for bringing this blessing to us, and we thank God every day for this wonderful opportunity. It's great helping other people; and the more we help them, the more we help ourselves.

"This business also gives us more quality time with our six-year-old son, Joshua, and that is more important than ever now.

"Through our new business, we have met and made wonderful friends, and have learned to build the self-confidence we need because we truly see the power of multilevel marketing.

"We are paid to help other people succeed. It is better to be paid a small percentage from a lot of other peoples' efforts, than to be paid 100% from your own. That is the quickest way to become financially secure. We are excited about the future of telecommunications—the information highway—and what it has in store for us.

"Life is about taking chances. We took a chance on

this business, and it is definitely paying off. We are in charge of our financial destiny. We have the freedom and family time we so desperately needed. We have the greatest support of all...our networking 'Family.' In the face of adversity, we have been truly blessed with the greatest business opportunity ever."

What a powerful story! It's hearing this message and others like it that inspires me to convince people that network marketing could be a blessing for them, as well. My special gift of selling fits perfectly. I discovered that I am not only a closer, but a motivator! I am able to help people believe in themselves.

chapter three

How Network Marketing Really Works

(And why I love it!)

Network marketing is people selling products and services by word of mouth, getting paid for it, and getting others to do the same. It's that simple.

Word of mouth has always been the best way to sell. Ask Hollywood. Ask the owner of the hot new restaurant in town. Ask MCI, whose "Friends and Family" program paid their customers (through reduced long-distance rates) to recruit new phone customers to their company. This is network marketing.

Remember the last time someone asked you to suggest a good book, or a good place to buy a dress, or a good deal on tires? You were network marketing. You just weren't getting *paid.*

However, by going through the same process for a network marketing company, you can actually earn part of the profits. By telling friends about your favorite vitamins, cosmetic products, or long distance service, you can earn money from doing what you already do every day.

But that's just the beginning. You also make money by sharing your business with friends.

When they begin selling the same products or services, you'll get a small percentage of the profits. Even better, as these new "representatives" sign up new reps, you'll make even MORE money, and on and on. This "downline" growth results in residual or "future" income as a result of your efforts today.

With network marketing, you have the hope—perhaps for the first time in your life—that you can one day stop working, but still have the income you need to enjoy life, to truly feast on the fruits of your labor.

What makes Network Marketing so wonderful

Unlimited income.

Think of the job you have right now, or the business you own. Think of the best possible scenario. How much more money can you possibly hope to earn a year from today? Assume you get the biggest raises, the best promotion, set a record for sales. How much more can you earn?

For most of us, no matter how hard we work or how lucky we are, our potential income is limited. It's limited by several factors but the most obvious is our job. When I was co-owner of a construction business, the best our business could possibly do in a year was to clear $100,000. That was it. If we sold every building, got every contract and worked 80-hour weeks, that was the top. Usually the income stream from the company was much lower than that.

For salaried workers potential income is usually even more limited. Since 1980, in fact, real incomes (after taking out inflation) have actually gone down for middle-income workers.

My last salaried position was with a pension administration firm. When they hired me as an actuarial assistant in 1980, I was a college graduate who had been to law school and had already owned a business. For this, they paid a grand sum of $15,000. After five years, I had advanced until I was answering only to the president—and was making $35,000. After bringing in $750,000 in revenues in a single deal, I asked for a raise based on my performance.

"I can't give you any more money!" the president insisted. "I'm only making $50,000. You'd be making more than I am!" OK, I countered, then let me have some stock in the company.

"I can't do that, either. I've got three sons, and that stock is their future."

Well, I had three sons, too, and I told him that I had to worry about their future. So I immediately made plans to start my own company.

When the president found out, he called me into his office and offered me a huge raise: $75,000 a year. "I couldn't do that," I demurred. "Why, I'd be making more than YOU."

The point is, no matter how hard you work, your employer is almost always going to constrain your income growth. They aren't necessarily trying to hurt you. They just have other priorities besides maximizing your salary.

But, as a worker, you have no limits on your desire to prosper and do well. There is no ceiling to dreams and aspirations. But in many jobs, there is a very definite ceiling on your potential income.

Ask yourself right now how much money you would like to be earning a year from today.

Now, ask yourself if there is even a remote possibility of coming close in your current job. If you are like most employees in America today, your future advancement and income possibilities are in no way linked to your actual efforts.

Therefore, you will never be paid what you're truly worth.

I had climbed up the income ladder to the "grandiose" salary of $35,000. I knew that I had maxed out in that company. Even if I had taken the $75,000 (and I'm not at all sure he wouldn't have reconsidered the next day!), there would have been serious problems among the executives in the company. Ultimately, I would have had to make the same decision—it was time to move on.

Paul Orberson, network marketing's Million-Dollar Man, says

it right: "Businesses pay you just enough so you won't quit. And you return the favor by doing just enough not to get fired."

Prospering from the efforts of others

When I left my $35,000 a year job and started my own company, I found out (the hard way) that owning your own company does free up your earning potential and allow you to earn money. It also gives you the freedom to set your own schedule and be your own boss.

But—and this is a huge BUT—it gives you a ton of added expenses and responsibilities.

First, you have to locate and rent an office (before, you just showed up at one). Then, you must get furniture, supplies, office equipment, etc. Then you must find someone trustworthy to work for you, and retain a CPA to do the accounting, withholding, tax filings and about a hundred other annoying duties.

Then you are free to set your schedule all right; you can choose to work between 60 and 80 hours a week! You never have to worry about selecting a time or place for your vacation, however, because you never get one. Sure, you are your own boss, but then again you are your own everything—you even get to be your own cleaning person!

I soon realized that, while owning my own small company had financial opportunities, that opportunity came with a myriad of responsibilities, hassles and burdens. It seemed most of the additional income went to workers' salaries or overhead.

I was looking for a way for other people to help me make more income. I decided I would start an insurance brokerage company and hire several agents to share the office space and expenses. I became a General Agent with a major life insurance company; then, I recruited agents to sign up under me to be trained and motivated in return for a percentage of the commission on all the policies they wrote.

The agents made 80% while I made 20%. That was great, but after I brought four agents into the company under my contract,

I spent all my selling time training and working with them.

Pretty soon I saw that they had a better deal than I did, and they had time to play golf, fish and vacation!

Network marketing was the perfect business for me. Though I have built a large organization of entrepreneurs who wanted to run their own business, I still continue to sell the telephone service and sponsor others to do the same. I receive income from my efforts as well as the efforts of my entire downline (the ones I sign up, and the ones they sign up, etc.)

Now, I admit I wouldn't make a lot of money if I had only four people in my downline, but that's just the point. You get the few you sign up a few more, and they get a few more, and you end up with thousands of people whom you make money on. You don't even know all the people. It's amazing!

Residual income

The most important aspect of network marketing and the main reason I think it is so wonderful is residual income. That is income generated after you stop working. It doesn't get much better than that!

In the insurance industry, we had a form of residual income called renewals. Every time one of our policy holders renewed (usually annually), we received a renewal commission, which was a very small percentage of the original premium for the policy. It took many years for the income to grow into a sizable amount, and you lost this income if the policy holder dropped the policy or died.

It was VERY frustrating—especially if you wrote huge groups of policies like I did. I wrote compensation plans for big corporations, so it was possible for 10 or 20 policies to be dropped all at once.

In network marketing, you sign up a few people (sponsor them) and teach them how to do the same. It's a business of duplication! In my business, I have personally signed up 26 customers, but I get residual income from approximately 75,000 customers. Imagine that!

Any time one of those 75,000 customers makes a long distance call, I get paid a tiny bit of commission.

Do you know, for instance, that Mother's Day is the busiest telephone usage day of the year?

Now I have much more to celebrate than my precious mother and my five great kids that day—I love residual income, and I truly love this business!

Origins of Network Marketing

After spending time in a Chinese prison camp in the 1920s, Dr. Carl Rehnborg, a renowned chemist, became interested in nutrition and invented a new food supplement derived from alfalfa, watercress, parsley, and various vitamins and minerals. He formed Nutrilite Products, Inc., to market his excellent new product. Today this company is a subsidiary of Amway Corporation.

Rehnborg is credited with developing the first network marketing plan. The company did not hire a sales force, but instead recruited a large number of independent representatives to sell the product. Rehnborg had no overhead or salary expense for his sales force because they were not employees—they were independent distributors. And he didn't even have to pay them commissions until after they had made a sale!

He had no training or recruiting headaches because the distributors took care of that, and the more distributors each distributor recruited, the more money they had, and the more Rehnborg made. His distributors only made commissions on their personal recruits—the people they recruited themselves. This company was a "single-level" company. Today, network marketing companies allow their distributors to draw commissions from several levels or "generations" of recruits. A distributor gets a percentage of sales from those who were recruited by his recruits, and so on. For this reason, network marketing is often called "multi-level marketing" or MLM for short.

The math behind the magic

Geometric progression is the power behind network marketing.

When distributors or independent representatives are paid commissions several levels down—that is, paid commissions on the sales of five, six or seven levels of distributors—the income can become sizable because the number of reps or distributors multiplies geometrically. For instance, if (A) recruits (B), (C), and (D) and those recruits each recruit three and those recruit three, etc., (A)'s business will look like the following:

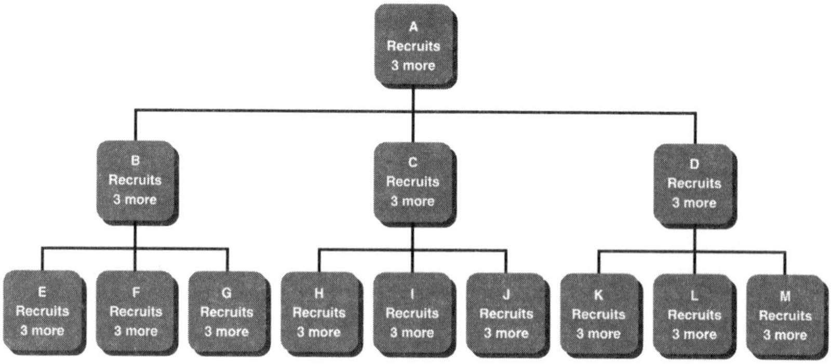

Geometric Progression of Network Marketing

(A) has three reps on his first level and nine reps on his second level. If each of the nine reps sponsored three more, there would be 27 on (A)'s third level, 81 on (A)'s fourth, etc.

The entire group above (and possibly other levels not shown, depending on the marketing plan of the specific company) would be (A)'s downline or organization.

(A) would be receiving income in varying amounts from each of the reps.

A network marketing business that follows all of the legal guidelines pertaining to this industry is the best vehicle available today for pursuing the American Dream. Franchising used to be an effective vehicle, but it has evolved into a sophisticated, big-business opportunity that is financially out of reach for the majority of Americans. Plus, operating a franchise requires a big time commitment. In other words, you might make money running a franchise business, but you will not be free.

In a network marketing business, you can work as many hours as you want, but you also know that many, many others are working under you and providing you a way to one day give up working completely. I admit the first couple of years in a network marketing company will require long hard hours, but you will know that it was worth it when the residual income keeps coming after you stop working.

Three ways you can make money from Network Marketing

1) Selling the product or service.

Network marketing companies know that the only way to hold on to loyal customers is to create a sales force of sales representatives or distributors who actually sell the products or service to their "warm market," to the people who will be loyal to them because of a relationship—family, friend or business.

These representatives usually buy the products at wholesale prices and resell them to this warm market at retail prices, keeping the difference as their profit. Most companies pay an additional commission or bonus in addition to the spread between retail and wholesale.

If the company offers a service, such as long distance telephone, the representatives receive a percentage of the long-distance monthly usage for each of the customers they sign up for the telephone service. It would take a large number of customers for each representative to make a significant amount of income because the average monthly long distance usage is only twenty-five to thirty dollars in the United States. Companies pay representatives a small percentage of that low long distance usage-somewhere from two to eight percent per month—so it would take a large number of customers to generate a significant income. If this were all the company offered in the way of income, no one would find financial security in network marketing.

2) Getting others to do the same: recruiting.

To add geometry to your business you need to be in a company that has more than one level of marketing—a multi-level marketing company (MLM).

Successful network marketing companies attract a very professional group of management-level people who act as sales representatives or distributors for their products or services. These representatives gather a small number of customers, and recruit and work with other representatives to develop an organization of customer gatherers. They are paid bonuses and commissions for developing and working with their organization to gather customers. These representatives can make money gathering customers personally, but they can earn a fortune by building a large organization of customer gatherers.

3) Relaxing when your work is done because of Residual Income.

Network marketing is the ultimate in residual income. Long after you move to the golf resort or cast off on your round-the-world cruise, your customers keep buying and your downline keeps selling, and you keep earning an income.

Network marketing allows your efforts today to continue to pay off for you tomorrow. This is a key element in achieving the American Dream. We all want to believe that the long hours and sacrifices we make today will do more than just "make ends meet" in the future.

We want the sacrifice of today to result in leisure and security in the long run.

Network marketing will be to the next few decades what franchising has been to the last three or four—an extremely popular and quite successful method of marketing goods and services.

Franchising had its difficult days in its infant stage because it was new and untried. At one point in its early years, franchising was almost outlawed by Congress. It was a mere 11 votes away from being declared illegal.

Early franchisees had to be daring and bold because they were constantly bombarded by the media—accused of hurting the little people! It amazes me how much the press likes to champion the less fortunate and the have-nots, because they think that is the politically correct thing to do. Yet, often the result is that they destroy the very entrepreneurial vehicles that might possibly be the only means these so-called have-nots will ever have to balance the scales of economic justice.

Fortunately, many adventurous risk-takers were willing to risk all, while the media, many government regulators, and much of the general public condemned them. Franchising was ultimately successful for one simple reason. The idea made sense!

Companies found they could grow much faster and more economically if they offered independent businessmen and women the opportunity to replicate the original company at the businessmen's expense rather than going into debt or incurring greater overhead to build multiple locations themselves. The better franchises not only require the independent businessmen to bear the start-up costs, but they charge a large fee for the privilege.

Franchising is now a well-respected form of marketing that accounts for over a third of all retail sales in our country. Many of the companies using franchising are among the highest rated on the New York Stock Exchange. This industry has survived its pioneering stage and is flourishing. And as it has gained respect and acceptance, it has also gained in value—market value, that is.

Unfortunately, many of the better franchises are priced significantly out of reach of average people. Today, franchising is big business—inaccessible to the average American, not the entrepreneurial vehicle it once was. Now, where does the little guy go? There's only one place left.

It's network marketing, a revolutionary new path to the oldest dream of all!

real-life stories

Michael Warshaw, Duncan Anderson

Success Magazine

When I began writing "The New American Dream," I sat down for a few minutes with Michael Warshaw and Duncan Anderson of *Success Magazine. Success* is a wonderful magazine for entrepreneurs and self-employed business owners—the "economic pioneers" of our day. *Success Magazine* has written extensively on network and multi-level marketing, helping to bring a new generation of white-collar professionals into the industry. I first spoke with Michael Warshaw when he called to interview me for their December 1995 issue, entitled, "We Create Millionaires."

Michael Warshaw is the Executive Editor of *Success,* and Duncan Anderson is the Network Marketing Editor. I began by asking them the most common question I get every day: "What *is* network marketing?"

Duncan: "Network marketing is a process where you become a distributor for a product, you find customers to buy your product, and some of those customers become distributors, too.

"When they do, you become, in effect, their sales manager, with a payment system very similar to 'overrides' paid to sales managers in other businesses. The difference is these overrides reach down more than one or two levels."

Betty: "Is it legitimate?"

Duncan: "Is $7.5 billion dollars legitimate? That's what Amway's sales will be in 1996. Or how about NuSkin and Forever Living, two network marketing companies that will do close to $1 billion in sales this year?"

Betty: "Then why does network marketing still have a questionable reputation in some circles?"

Duncan: "It's true that people don't really understand network marketing. They don't understand how much the industry has changed. When people get started in network marketing their friends and colleagues often treat them like they've become addicted to a new drug: 'OK, Joe, everyone goes through these stages, but don't worry. We'll help you work it out.' It's a step away from what they understand."

Michael: "Entrepreneurs know something that other people don't know. The old social model is based on the notion that wealth is limited. Entrepreneurs know that wealth is created. When someone does network marketing successfully, they are creating wealth—certainly for themselves, but also for their lines, up and down."

Duncan: "And more and more professionals are beginning to understand. People in white collar jobs with six figure salaries are getting involved. You talk to people in sales, in marketing, in the medical profession, lawyers, whatever. You'll hear stories of people they know personally who got tired of the rat race, who weren't having fun any more, and who have decided to go into network marketing."

Betty: "Does network marketing really work?"

Duncan: "Yes. People make money selling their products, the customers like the products they buy, and the company makes money doing it. Network marketing works."

Betty: "OK, Duncan, then *why* does it work?"

Duncan: "Look at the products that are especially popular in network marketing: vitamins, personal and health care products, nutritional supplements. These products need explanation. There's something to explain.

"Network marketing is the opposite of a retail shelf. People need to hear about the product, and they need to hear information the manufacturer cannot give. Does ginseng really work?

"I don't know, but I knew my neighbor BEFORE she started taking it. Now, she's healthier and happier. Am I going to listen when she recommends what she's taking? You bet."

Michael: "Network marketing is a personal business. There are people who couldn't do commissioned sales because they aren't professionally motivated.

"But the same people, once they become product motivated, will sell everyone they know the product that has worked for them. They aren't afraid to talk about a product they use and really like. These people are very powerful recruiters for the company. Then you have people who can recruit others who are really powerful."

Betty: "So, when does network marketing fail?"

Duncan: "There are many reasons why some people don't do well in network marketing. It's difficult to keep at it, for one thing. The rewards come after a lot of investment of time and effort, with little or no gain at the beginning.

"Some people never get used to selling. They're uncomfortable talking to strangers. Maybe they just can't get used to the notion of not having a 'real' job; the way of life doesn't appeal to them. And sometimes the company itself is a problem: it's not well run, or fails to deliver products on time, or is just plain dishonest."

Betty: "How can I make sure I'm dealing with a good network marketing company?"

Duncan: "From a legal standpoint, just ask some enterprising law student to find out if the individuals running the company have ever been sued or imprisoned.

"From a financial standpoint, you want a company that is growing, one that is on the move.

"Talk to distributors, get a feel for the company's success. Be sure to compare several companies and their compensation plans. For example, a 'breakaway' plan is better for people who are working the program full-time and are very self-motivated. A 'unilevel' compensation plan is usually better for part-time people; it's more rewarding for lower levels of sales, but there's less potential at the high end."

Betty: "What is the future of network marketing?"

Michael: "The future is very bright when you consider the people who are getting into the industry. They are professional, white-collar people, people with options. They don't need network marketing. But they see the opportunity and, by getting involved, they are changing the perception of the industry."

Duncan: "Network marketing is only going to go one way: up. There are so many things that can be sold through networking: financial services, Internet services, even electrical power. Right now, traditional long distance companies are very worried about network companies in their industry. Four of the top 20 personal care products today are network marketing companies.

"Network marketing is here to stay. Every company that is serious about the future should look at network marketing. If they don't, I can guarantee someone else will."

real-life stories

Mickey & Leslie Tumlin

Mickey and Leslie Tumlin are perfect examples of over-achievers who one day want to stop working. They have a higher goal of achieving the financial freedom they need so they can share with the world their deep sense of missionary work.

Mickey Tumlin sets his goals high.

As a member of the 1971 Sanford University football team, he experienced the joy of winning a national championship in Division II. It's an experience he still thinks of fondly.

In 1976, he started his own pharmacy at the age of 26, the youngest pharmacist to do so in his home state of Alabama. He likes to remember that accomplishment.

He also remembers a less positive experience, his involvement with a network (or multi-level) marketing company years ago, a company that eventually went under. "It left a bitter taste in my mouth," says Mickey. "I took 18 months away from my work on my pharmacies, and the company just folded and walked away with my money."

But as I mentioned, Mickey sets high goals. He and his wife, Leslie, saw very clearly the potential of network marketing, despite a bad experience. Indeed, Leslie, who has a business degree from the University of Alabama at Birmingham, eventually got involved with several other network marketing companies.

"I did commissioned sales for a while—the worst job anyone could ever have, in my opinion.

"Then I spent 11 years as a full-time mom. I got involved with some multi-level companies, but without any lofty goals. I wanted to buy the products at cost and maybe make a little money," says Leslie.

Meanwhile, Mickey was experiencing the joys of owning his own chain of pharmacies.

"An independent pharmacist is more than a pharmacist; you're a business manager, an office manager, a psychologist. Many times I would be doing paperwork at 12:30 or 1:00 at night, then get back up at 6:00 to run the pharmacy."

For Mickey and Leslie, the elusive dream was always of building a lasting business that would allow them to stop working, but still earn a strong income. "We both believed network marketing could work, but only with the right company. I wanted the freedom of time, and I've always had a performance-based personality, which is a plus in the network marketing business. But for a long time, it didn't come together."

Mickey and Leslie remind me why it is so important to keep asking people about getting involved, even if they've always said no or have tried some other company. You never know when you'll finally make the right match.

"We were invited to a meeting, and we went. We were open-minded but cautious," says Leslie. "Mickey came out with tempered enthusiasm. I came out energized. I was ready to get started. Mickey said he wanted to take his time and look at it, but I never saw him looking.

So finally I said, 'That's it. I'm going to sign up.'

"A couple of weeks later, I packed our house with 40 people and every one of them signed up. That got Mickey's attention, and we were off to the races."

They now have a large and prospering downline, along with a very generous income. They work the business as a team.

"Mickey has started a business before, and I have a background in sales, so it's a very good fit," says Leslie. "Mickey is a good coach, he knows how to motivate people."

Mickey looks for the willingness to be coached when he signs up representatives: "They have to be coachable, be willing to learn, and they have to believe in me, as their coach," says Mickey. "But the number one characteristic in people who succeed is drive, determination."

"My drive comes from watching my father as I grew up. He was a steelworker and a full-time pastor. He gave and gave of himself, and he pushed me to do better than he did."

"We never went hungry but we didn't have much money, and I remember very distinctly, hot August nights in Alabama, lying sweaty in my bed and thinking that if I ever got cool again, I would stay that way. So I know what it's like to be hungry for something, to have the drive to do better. That drive can't be coached. It has to be felt."

As a network marketer, Leslie's reward comes in seeing the attitude of success: "We look for people who are living the outcome, whose attitude toward those who doubt them is 'Just watch me!' They know what they're going to achieve and they're doing it. They're living it before it even happens. It's just a matter of time," says Leslie.

Not everyone succeeds, of course. "The people who fail at network marketing are the ones who want something for nothing," says Mickey. "They're the ones who allow small things to defeat them. They have pie-in-the-sky dreams. They've attached their dream to someone else and they aren't willing to do the work themselves."

Leslie always reminds their reps that network marketing is very different from traditional business. "It requires an awful lot of patience. The rewards come later. In commissioned sales, you make a sale, you get the check in thirty days. You make the big sale, you get a check, you get a plaque, you get recognition.

"In network marketing, you make a deal and get people in the business, and it's six months before you get your reward. It's hard to keep people motivated for those rewards in our society's current focus on immediate gratification."

That may be society's focus, but it's not Mickey and Leslie's.

Their motto is "Excel in the Grace of Giving," and they are. "A big goal of ours is to take 300 of our company's reps on a mission trip to Bulgaria and Romania. We want to give back, we want to make a difference.

And it's going to happen."

The Tumlins will make it happen!

chapter four

Why Network Marketing is right for you!

(And me, too!)

Being introduced to network marketing can be frustrating because the answers to many of the questions asked by reps are obvious: we all want more income, more hope and the chance for financial freedom. As my father used to say, "If wishes were horses, beggars would ride!"

Five key elements of Network Marketing

Just because network marketing works for others, does that mean it's right for you? There are five key benefits of network marketing that have made it the fastest and easiest way for everyday people to achieve the American dream. Review them and consider giving network marketing the opportunity to change your life.

1) Low start-up costs

Have you priced a franchise lately? Unbelievable! The great ones require several hundred thousand dollars to get started; the good ones are at least $100,000, and even the not-so-good ones are $10–$20,000. Most people just can't come up with that kind of money.

But in network marketing, even the great companies require practically no start-up costs. In fact, if a multi-level or network marketing company requires a substantial amount up front, you better check its legal status. You can actually get in to most of these companies for a couple of hundred dollars, and even that is usually optional. This money is used for supplies, brochures, sales aids, home office support, newsletters and—most importantly—a financial report of your sales activities.

I love the idea of offering people with little or no income or savings the opportunity to begin their own business without getting into additional debt. Most Americans struggle financially their entire lives and retire with a dread of outliving their meager retirement income.

Imagine, in a land of great prosperity, many citizens facing their twilight years asking themselves, "Will I live too long? What if the money runs out?"

According to an article by Louis Richman in *Fortune* magazine, it's not only the older generation that is anxiety-ridden:

> "Today a queasy sense of insecurity haunts many working people. From neatly-coifed executives to aproned production workers, once secure futures now seem threatened. Wave after wave of corporate restructurings has knocked away the underpinnings of career-long employment that sustained workers' confidence in their future."

2) Unlimited earnings potential

Network marketing provides the vehicle for achieving a wide range of income levels, from a few hundred dollars a month part-time as supplemental income, to a six-figure or even more, full-time income. The right network marketing opportunity can provide as much cash flow as you are willing to work for. There is no ceiling. And the residual income will allow you to retire without the fear of outliving your income or your savings.

Most people get involved in a network marketing opportunity

to earn some "extra" money to supplement the income from their regular job. If they make a commitment to give 100% during the limited time they spend on their new business, many will soon realize that they can achieve the same income level, working part-time, as they were earning at their regular job.

At that point, it's time to make a decision.

If a limited number of hours will produce the same income as the full-time job, what could be accomplished if the network marketing were a full-time job?

Network marketing offers more freedom, more excitement and more job satisfaction because it not only changes the marketer's life, it changes the lives of everyone involved. In network marketing, the more you help others, the more successful you are. This is in stark contrast to regular jobs with their get-others-out-of-your-way, take-credit-for-those-ideas attitude that makes you more likely to climb over your peers than lift them up.

3) No special skills required

No special skills or attributes are required to succeed in network marketing. Some talents may make it work easier, but no one attribute is necessary.

• *Age is not a factor.*

I have an 84-year-old lady in my organization. She's a delightful person, and people love working for her. Her age is not a handicap; in fact, I'd say it is an asset. She is admired and respected by her entire hometown, and this business is giving her life a whole new dimension.

She is interested in the long-term residual income, since she may want to stop working someday!

• *Sex is not a factor.*

Network marketing attracts men and women, and it works very well for either. It works even better if a couple does it together. Since it can be time-consuming if done on a full-time basis, many husbands and wives enjoy working their business together in order to have exciting and meaningful time with each other. Sometimes, one spouse will work the network marketing business while the other continues in a full-time conventional job.

There are more women in network marketing than men—primarily because women seem to adapt to this method of marketing more rapidly than men. I believe women are natural nurturers. It's a gift from God. Nurturing your downline is necessary for success.

• *Race is not a factor.*

Network marketing transcends all racial barriers. When a person is looking for a new representative to sponsor, they only care about the ability to duplicate; that is, get a few others to do what they are doing.

• *Education is not a factor.*

Bob Diseker, a Ph.D. in Winston-Salem, North Carolina, never imagined he would be in network marketing. He is a financial planner who specializes in structuring plans for his clients that will enable them to retire comfortably. He makes recommendations of various investment strategies and estate planning techniques that help create and preserve enough income to provide for their needs and as many luxuries as possible. He does this through wise investments and prudent tax planning.

Bob is greatly respected and admired, and many people have joined our company because of his impeccable financial discernment and unquestionable integrity. But, he decided he would like to retire one day, instead of spending his whole life showing others how to do it. He signs up most of his reps in one-on-one office meetings and at luncheons. His style of marketing and recruiting is a little more sophisticated than mine but he does very well.

Others in my organization have only a few years of education, but they too are successful. Their self-esteem is greatly enhanced by the admiration and support of their downline.

Network marketing represents a team effort. No one individual operating alone could be this successful. Therefore, an individual leader gets credit and recognition for finding and motivating the group.

Lois Eargle, a dear friend in Conway, South Carolina, didn't have the opportunity for a formal education, but she never let that slow her down. She and her husband, Jack, struggled to send their five children to college.

Lois served our state in the House of Representatives for eight years and was the assistant to the Secretary of State for several years before being elected auditor in her home county.

She's one of the most popular women in South Carolina, and it would not surprise me if she became the first female governor of this state.

Even though she was incredibly successful in her professional life, she was never able to earn the income that she deserved—not even close—until she decided to try network marketing. It only took a few months part-time to match the income she was receiving from the state of South Carolina, and she has helped many others improve their financial situation at the same time.

• *Sales experience is not a factor.*

Many salesmen are attracted to network marketing. It doesn't hurt to have had sales training and experience, but it isn't a prerequisite. The experience might make it a little easier to approach prospects initially, but it certainly isn't necessary to close the sale. I would even argue that bringing in reps is not "selling" in the traditional sense, but rather, "sorting," to find individuals who see the value of the opportunity.

4) Flexibility

Network marketing can be a full-time or a part-time job. It can take one hour a day, one day a week, or one day a month. It's flexible. If you have to stop for a short time, you can. One neat aspect of network marketing is discovering people in your downline who choose to work the business full-time. Their efforts help you—especially if they sign up a few others who want to do what they are doing.

When my husband Jim was running for re-election, I had to take off from my business for three months to help with his campaign. My business continued and so did my income. It was easy for me to pick up where I left off because my downline had been busy keeping the business going while I was away. Since I had no overhead and no employees, I had not run up any big expenses, and I received checks the entire time I was out. What a business!

5) Residual income

Residual income is the money you make after you stop working. It's the magic of network marketing! How many jobs offer this type of income? Retirement plans pay you after you stop working, but usually only a percentage of the income you received while actively employed. And some retirement income you can outlive.

Conclusion

In conclusion, let me reiterate that anyone regardless of their age, race, sex, education, current financial condition, current employment, or even their physical condition, in most cases, can do this business.

The telecommunications company I'm involved in has several blind people excitedly and effectively working this business, a couple of quadriplegics, a large group of hearing impaired (many meetings have signers) and some who have been disabled for many years.

I was at a meeting recently in Myrtle Beach, South Carolina, and a young man in his late teens approached me, overflowing with praise for the company and his business. He had already advanced to a top level position and his eyes were sparkling as he shared his story with me.

After he walked away, his father whispered to me, "You'd never know he was legally blind, would you?" I shook my head—I was truly amazed. I honestly couldn't tell.

Then I was shocked again the next evening when a pretty lady came up to me and said that her daughter was dating the young man from Myrtle Beach and she (the daughter) was legally blind, too, and working in this telecommunications business herself. What an inspiration!

Can't you see how this could be the perfect business for just about anyone? You don't need a lot of money to get started, so it doesn't matter if you're rich or poor. You can earn as much as you choose to work for or have a part-time income for those extras you've never quite had enough left over to get. You can do it anywhere and at anytime. You don't need sales experience or a certain level of education and it doesn't matter what your race, age or sex is. And most importantly, you can stop worrying about retirement. You will be able to have one, after all.

real-life stories

Kathy Inabinet Laney

Networking is the most satisfying and rewarding business you can be in because the more you give, the more you get. Basically, this industry rewards the biggest hearts with the biggest bucks. Kathryn Inabinent Laney is living proof. She has a big heart, but she is anything but your stereotypical network marketer. In fact, she's not a stereotypical anything.

Kathy grew up on a South Carolina plantation, surrounded by magnolias, crepe myrtle and money. Her father owned a large and successful company and sent his daughter to prestigious Mary Baldwin College in Stanton, Virginia. She even once worked in Senator Strom Thurmond's office.

Her first job was director of advertising for her father's company. But when he passed away, the company was sold and Kathy decided to enter the ministry.

"My father was a tremendous man," says Kathy. "He was 6'7" and played professional football for the

Baltimore Colts. He taught me to pursue life with abandon, to follow your heart, and he had been very successful. His death sent me on a path of self-discovery and soul-searching."

Her searching led Kathy to a Masters of Divinity from Emory University and a new career as a minister in the United Methodist church. She served in the church for seven years, but felt a yearning for even more.

"The dream of my heart was to be financially free, but still serve others. I wanted to find a way to use what a friend calls my 'gifts and graces' to help people prosper both spiritually and financially. I found it in network marketing.

"A friend introduced me to a long distance networking company and said, 'Kathy, this is you.'

"Believe it or not, I had never been exposed to network marketing before. I suppose that's because I grew up in a fairly affluent family, everyone thought we wouldn't be interested. But I saw the tremendous potential."

Many of us make the same mistake. We know people who are professional or business owners or just plain old rich, and we assume they aren't interested in new opportunities. But network marketing can be a tremendous benefit to anyone.

Not everyone sees the opportunities, however.

Kathy continues, "When I was first getting started, I signed up a woman from an affluent family in a very nice neighborhood. She was so excited to have a way to earn money and help her friends. But when her husband heard about it, he demanded that I tear up his wife's check. He said he was ashamed at the thought of his wife being involved in network marketing.

"To make things worse, he didn't have the nerve to call me himself, so he had his wife call and relay his message. We both felt awful. I even cried.

"But then, I took a deep breath and got back to work. I realized that he was the one who should be crying. He had missed his opportunity."

Making the move from pastor to network marketing may

seem like a drastic change but Kathy doesn't see it that way.

"The relationship between myself and my downline is similar to my relationship with a congregation. I'm trying to motivate people, to be positive, to create hope for the future and faith in themselves. Sometimes I need to fuss at them a little when they get off track. But the goal is the same—I'm always trying to make a difference in people's lives."

Kathy is a perfect example of how network marketing can bring positive change to your life, how it can broaden your horizon of hope.

"I ask people who are looking at network marketing two questions:

'Are you happy with your job?' And 'what are you doing for the community?' To me, getting rich while those around you are still struggling isn't what it's all about. I believe we have a duty to help others build better lives for themselves. Network marketing allows you to do this while building a financially secure future for yourself."

Kathy worked for a while as a chaplain in a state mental health agency and saw first hand the tremendous toll poverty and hopelessness can have on people's lives.

"When you think about how little it takes to change a life, it's truly amazing," says Kathy.

"For many people, $300 a month means quality day care for their children. $500 a month is a new home. The effects of this income on the personal, spiritual and family lives of real people is almost immeasurable."

For special people like Kathy Laney, personal wealth and social position are not enough.

They want to reach out to others, to help people find a way to take care of their families, to be happier, more free, and more prosperous. Network marketing may be the only business with an opportunity as big as Kathy Laney's heart.

real-life stories

Dr. Gene Bass

Most people think doctors have it made when they get through with their studies and start practicing. But talk to a few doctors and you'll hear a different story: tremendous debt from medical school, the expenses of operating a business, the pressures of their practice. Then, after working terrible hours, never seeing their families, and hassling with tons of governmental red tape, they can't even enjoy their retirement because of the prohibitive cost of tail premiums on their malpractice policies and insufficient retirement incomes.

Dr. Gene Bass of Long Beach, Mississippi, has found the best medicine for professionals who are ready to pull out of the rat race: network marketing.

"Today I see a lot of people in different professions who have done well, but stress, litigation and paperwork are driving them away from their work. They want to change, but they are shackled by golden handcuffs. They aren't prepared to throw away an entire career, and even if they were, they can't afford the loss of income. I'm a perfect example: I had practically two college educations, plus four years of med school, a year of internship, four years residence and a six-months sports medicine fellowship. You hate to throw that away."

Especially a medical education that Dr. Bass almost didn't get. "I had already graduated college, I was teaching and coaching at the high school level. I had played college football and I enjoyed coaching, but I met a CPA one day who was going back to school hoping to get into med school. I thought, "Hey, I could do that." So I made a deal with my wife that I would take one year of pre-med courses, and if I did well, I would apply to medical school at the University of Mississippi."

While a medical student and intern, Gene Bass was also a husband and father. He saw early on the toll a doctor's life can take on his family. "That's one reason I pursued orthopedic surgery as a specialty. It allows me to keep somewhat regular hours, to be with my family."

Dr. Bass also saw early on that medicine is a business, the bills have to be paid, and—like most professions—you are paid only for what you do, not what you start. "Network marketing is attractive to me because I can trade linear income (medical work) for residual income, which will pay me over and over again for the work I do today.

"I knew I needed a business that would keep earning income for me after I stopped working.

"I think we all do. We're the first generation that has faced the 'Triple Whammy' of having to pay for our children's college, take care of our elderly parents and save for our own retirement...all at the same time! Most of the people I know are not prepared, we haven't saved enough.

"So, a few years ago I was thinking of buying a franchise. I've never been fond of franchising because it costs so much up front—franchising fees, royalties, special training for employees.

"Then you still have all the same problems every small business owner faces, dealing with employees and supplies. I wasn't looking for ANOTHER headache with all the paperwork I've already got.

"One day I was looking over a franchising magazine at the bookstore and I happened to see an article on network marketing. Betty Miles was on the cover, and after reading the article I tracked her down and gave her a call. After listening to her talk about her opportunity, I thought to myself, 'This could be it.' And I was right."

Dr. Bass now runs a thriving network marketing business along with his medical practice.

Many of his reps are other professionals who have felt the same time and financial pressures Dr. Bass has experienced.

"When I hear someone talking about stress, about long hours, about fear of litigation or the burdens of work, I know they need to hear about my business," says Dr. Bass. "They need this hope. When people are worried about retirement, about paying for their kid's education—when they see that triple whammy—I know the best way I can help them is to show them this opportunity.

"More and more professionals, particularly in medicine, are re-thinking their careers. I've made a good living in medicine, but I have a lot of uncertainty about my future. Medicine is going through the equivalent of corporate downsizing, and so are many other professions."

This influx of experienced, self-motivated people is helping new network marketing businesses take off, and it is improving the public perception of the industry.

"Professionals don't think of themselves as salespeople. I don't think of it as selling, it's just showing an opportunity. If people aren't looking for opportunity, it doesn't matter what you say. They aren't going to make this work," says Dr. Bass.

"I'm very fortunate. I've found a company and a product I'm comfortable with. I enjoy working with the telecommunications industry, and I'm enthusiastic about getting others involved. And unlike franchising, I've been able to start a business for about the price of a car payment, a business with no inventory, no deliveries, no collections and no employees. I still have my medical practice, I have my network marketing business, and I honestly believe that I am helping improve lives with both of them."

chapter five

But is it legal?

The single most common question I hear from people who know nothing about network marketing is the question "Isn't that a pyramid scheme?"

This is actually a good question because there are, in fact, pyramids and other scams popping up every day. And it gives me the opportunity to explain, clearly and carefully, how the network marketing industry truly works. However, no explanation can completely remove the stigma that network marketing has in the minds of some people.

For example, my husband Jim was opposed to my participation in any type of network marketing business, and he didn't hesitate to express his sentiments. But I was so excited about the opportunity I saw with my business that I pleaded with him to examine the company objectively before he made a judgment. Being a fair person, that's exactly what he did.

Jim admits now, "My initial reaction when Betty got involved with multi-level marketing was skepticism. I was apprehensive because of my preconceived notions about multi-level marketing. I remembered the chain letter craze which swept America when I was a child.

"My prejudices had led me to conclude, at first blush, that all multi-level marketing plans were bad. But that turned out not to be the case."

Jim began investigating the company I was considering. He did background checks on the owners and investigated the legal aspects of the marketing plan. His diligence was so thorough it was almost embarrassing. I was afraid that by the time he finished, the company wouldn't want me around anymore. But the more he checked the company, the better they seemed to like it.

And the more Jim liked them, too. After weeks of research, he quietly went to our 22-year-old son and said, "I think this may be the best money-making opportunity you'll ever have in your lifetime, son." When I heard that, I knew I was on to something big!

Still, questions remain for many people. As is often the case, the laws and regulations are running behind the pace of innovation. I like to compare current direct and multi-level marketing laws to the rules of the road that existed when the first automobiles began to appear.

When the automobile began turning heads a century ago, there was no such thing as a speed limit. Traffic laws were written for horse-drawn carriages, and they couldn't possible anticipate the problems created by motorcars. Indeed, the first uniform traffic guidelines for "motor carriages" weren't even written until almost a decade after the appearance of cars.

In the interim, some careless drivers gave cars a bad reputation with Americans who were more familiar with the peaceful pace of horse-and-buggy travel. They didn't understand this new vehicle, and they weren't sure they liked it, either.

Similarly, it has taken some years before many of the legal issues surrounding multi-level marketing became clear, but one thing is evident: Multi-level marketing of products and service *is* legal. But that doesn't mean that you shouldn't carefully examine any plan you are considering. Jim and I sure did!

When people talk about "pyramid schemes," they really mean

"Ponzi schemes." Ponzi schemes are illegal. A Ponzi scheme is named after Mr. Charles Ponzi. In the 1920s, Ponzi raised money from investors by promising to pay a 50% return on investments and, for a while, he did. He was able to pay these enormous returns by taking money from new investors and giving it to the old ones...after taking a generous portion himself. The pyramid eventually collapsed when Ponzi could not find new investors. Once no new capital could be found, the early investors could not be paid because there was no actual "investment." Nothing of value, no product or service was being produced by Ponzi with the investments. The only product being sold by Ponzi was empty promises!

An illegal Ponzi scheme generally has two characteristics—fraud and the absence of a tangible business enterprise. In a Ponzi scheme, the second investor in the scheme pays the interest to the first. The third investor pays the interest to the first and second investor, and so on. In pure Ponzi schemes, there are, literally, no products being sold. There are questions you can ask to make sure you are not getting involved in a Ponzi-style network marketing plan.

When you are researching a network marketing plan, ask these questions:

1) Is the multi-level marketing plan product or service driven?

If the plan relies on the sale of products or services to generate revenues, it passes the first test. If you find yourself forever recruiting new members to generate income, there may be a problem.

2) Does the plan give you unrefundable inventory?

Part of the stigma of network marketing comes from a handful of companies (now long defunct) that profited by forcing reps to buy large amounts of product upfront. The company was then guaranteed to make money even if the rep never sold a single thing. Most modern, legitimate multi-level marketing plans make a strong effort to avoid dumping products onto participants. Look for plans which do not require you as the seller to absorb the costs of unsold inventory.

3) Is the initial fee to participate outrageous?

Multi-level marketing plans should not be expensive to join. Beware of companies with large upfront fees.

4) Are products or services sold to other plan participants, or are they sold to retail customers?

Legitimate multi-level marketing plans sell to retail customers. They are a way to distribute products or services to the consumer marketplace with lower costs. Question plans which focus sales efforts only to club members or plan participants.

5) Will you make a million dollars a month without lifting a finger?

If it sounds too good to be true, it probably is! Multi-level marketing has brought the American dream to many Americans, but it takes effort! The advantage of multi-level marketing is that you are captain of your own destiny. You may work tirelessly for a Fortune 500 company for years and never reach the American Dream. If you devote the same effort to your multi-level marketing business, you will usually achieve financial freedom and more.

If you are interested in the particular court cases that governing network marketing, you may want to read *Appendix A* in the back of this book. But the main point you need to understand is that network and multi-level marketing represent the next wave of product distribution. These innovative forms of marketing take advantage of significant cost savings resulting from the absence of expensive advertising budgets and huge floods of investment capital. And, as it was for cars a century ago, these vehicles for economic opportunity are here to stay.

Time and time again, the legitimacy of multi-level marketing has been validated. Any plan which fits within these broad guidelines is worth exploring.

Most importantly, look at the product or service being sold. After all, it isn't worth investing your time and money if the product or service isn't worthwhile. If you decide that the multi-level marketing plan sells products or services to the retail marketplace at a competitive price, requires your efforts to succeed, and does not leave you stuck with inventories of unsold goods, then you may want to consider this latest way to achieve financial freedom.

Like the automobile a century ago, there might not be quite as many multi-level marketing distributors as there are old-fashioned stores. And you might hear some complaints from the old storekeepers. They might not like the pace of these new vehicles to the American Dream. But remember, multi-level marketing can get you to the American Dream faster than the old-fashioned way. The ride is also a lot more fun!

real-life stories

Ray Faltinsky

Ray Faltinsky is the only person I've met who was so excited by the opportunity of network marketing that he started his own company.

If ever there was a man who didn't need to go into network marketing, it is Ray Faltinsky.

As a successful student at the prestigious Yale Law School, Ray could write his own ticket to almost any major law firm in America.

But Ray had something else in mind. "My parents came to America in 1955. Neither of them spoke English and they had no money. My Dad worked as many as three jobs at one time, my mother raised four children and worked at a bakery, but they never gained their financial security. I'm not talking about becoming millionaires, just getting to the place where they didn't have to worry about being able to pay the rent."

Ray wanted to know what hard-working people without much money could do to have a chance to achieve lasting wealth and a secure financial future.

"My professors at Yale told

me that franchising was the answer, and maybe it once was. But most franchising opportunities involve relatively high start-up costs and franchising fees. For most people on modest incomes, $10,000 is more than they can afford."

Then, in 1990, Ray read an article about network marketing. A law student at the time, Ray wrote his thesis on the legal aspects of the network approach. His curiosity was aroused.

"Network marketing has the five key elements I was looking for," says Ray. "Low start up costs, unlimited earnings potential, a business that could be done part-time with no special skills, and a business that offers the opportunity to work less in the future, while your income continues to grow."

However, Ray's first experience with network marketing was not positive. "The first company I worked with required representatives to buy products up-front, and the marketing structure could have been better, in my opinion. As a result, I got my friends involved, I got my wife involved, and we all got stuck with the products. I almost gave up."

But he didn't. Ray believes that people who have had bad experiences with network marketing in the past are making a mistake by giving up on the industry.

"It's like going to a bad Italian restaurant," Ray says. You don't say 'I'm never going out for Italian food again.' You keep looking until you find a restaurant that does it right!"

And Ray kept looking, but when he couldn't find a company that was doing it his way, he did what millions of other business people have done: he started his own!

"FreeLife International brings together my lifelong interest in nutrition and health with my belief in network marketing. When I started FreeLife, there weren't many 'uni-level' companies. And most of the businesses were set up for full-time, not part-time, people. I wanted to create the ultimate marketing plan that would work for anyone, full-time or part-time. That's why FreeLife was created."

FreeLife International was

born in 1993, and three years later, had grown into a $10 million company. As of this writing, Ray's highest producer was earning $40,000 a month. What are his suggestions for people interested in network marketing?

"Watch out for front-end loading, companies that require you to purchase large amounts of products up-front. And while network marketing does offer unlimited income potential, be leery of unsubstantiated earnings claims. You want to talk to real people in the company in your area, and find out what they are making.

"And don't try to re-invent the wheel. Successful network marketing companies will show you tried-and-true methods for success. They want you to succeed, and so do the people in your upline. Let them help. Listen. And don't be afraid to ask questions.

"If you have a background in sales, network marketing is a very different approach. It's not like 'closin' the deal.' Using high-pressure sales to get a one-time sale is shortsighted. You want people who will go out and share your vision."

What does Ray think is the single most important key to success in network marketing?

"Persistence. Don't expect to be making big bucks in two or three months. It takes time and persistence. For the first few months in network marketing, you are vastly underpaid for the work you put in. But because of residual income and geometric growth, soon you will be vastly OVERPAID for the effort you put in.

"Network marketing is the ultimate delayed gratification. It doesn't come to you until way down the road. Selfish people don't do well. Short attention span multi-level marketing junkies never make money. You can't do it that way.

"But if you are persistent in your work and passionate about your product, you will succeed," Ray says.

With a legal education from Yale Law School, Ray's strong belief in network marketing corroborates my own view that this industry is for me!

real-life stories

Lloyd & Peggy Morris

That's what happened to Peggy and Lloyd Morris. They know first-hand how businesses work—and how a business can work *you.*

"I always wanted to build houses, even when I was a kid," says Lloyd, a veteran Army helicopter pilot. "But when I got out of the Army and opened my own contracting business, I found out that building houses on 'spec' involved high risk and low reward."

The hard work continued, according to his wife, Peggy, when they went into the real estate business. "When we sold real estate together, for ten years we had to work all day, seven days a week, with hardly ever a day off. If we did try to get away for a day, there was always a phone or pager nearby, because in real estate, you can lose a million dollar sale overnight."

Lloyd and Peggy were considered "successful" in real estate.

They enjoyed several years of $1 million plus sales. But the hours, the pressure and the relentless effort was wearing them down. They decided to take a look at network marketing.

"I heard Donald Trump say on *The Tonight Show* that, if he had it to do all over again, he would get into network marketing. That was enough to get our attention."

They examined numerous network marketing companies and programs, eventually signing up with Watkins, Inc., a home products company. "I wanted to distribute a real product, one that is necessary in everyday life," says Lloyd. "I didn't want to sell some 'luxury item' because when money gets tight, the first thing the customer cuts is YOU. I was raised on Watkins, I saw it as a kid. When I found out they were network marketing, I was sold."

As experienced business people, Peggy and Lloyd understand well the pragmatic, day-to-day business aspects of network marketing. They have very specific sales goals and a clear business plan.

"Our son and his wife worked with us and we can give this business to them one day, or we can sell it. This isn't 'pie-in-the-sky.' It's a real business based on retail sales," says Peggy, who estimated they will do $5 million in sales in 1996.

Lloyd and Peggy also appreciate the opportunity to be their own bosses. Both of their parents owned their own businesses. "I've always been self employed," says Peggy. And Lloyd says he "never even considered working for someone else."

"In network marketing, you are you own boss," says Peggy. "And if you work at it you can make a lot of money. You can also satisfy a basic need you have—to help others—and get paid for it.

"If you don't help people, you won't make money."

Lloyd agrees: "In the construction business it's dog-eat-dog. That's completely different from network marketing, where you get paid to help other people make sales."

"One thing sticks out in my mind," says Peggy. "We sponsored some people who were desperate—who had to max out their credit cards to get started. Later, after their business started growing, they called back and the mother in this family told me, 'I just bought a new dress. I want you to know that, for the first time as an adult, I didn't feel guilty about buying myself a new dress.' "

What advice do Lloyd and Peggy have for people considering a career in network marketing? They suggest:

"Like in any business, companies can quickly come and go. We recommend working with businesses that are at least 10 years old. Watch out for the supposed hot opportunity; that is folly. If it is a good deal now, it will be a good deal five or ten years from now.

"Think about how much inventory you have to handle, how much product you have to keep on hand. We could never hit the $5 million sales mark if we had to handle and distribute each item. The classic way network marketing should work is for you to handle the marketing and for the company to handle the product.

"While you can start in many network marketing businesses with little or no upfront money, we like to see people with maybe $1,000 to invest into their business. This gives you an early marketing edge.

"And learn to use a computer. This is essential in any business!"

Finally: "The best network marketers are self-motivated. They are able to get outside their comfort zone and 'go for it!' There has got to be motivation to achieve success. If you really want it, it's going to happen to you."

real-life stories

Lee Simonson

My husband is one of the few true statesmen I have known, but several months ago, I was contacted by another one. When Lee Simonson called me from 1500 miles away to ask me about my network marketing experiences, I could tell he was the kind of person who doesn't do things halfway.

After less than 2 months in the business, here's his plan:

"We're going to take over Niagara County, one customer at a time." And he means it, too.

Lee is a lifetime entrepreneur. His parents ran a photography studio out of their home when he was growing up, and Lee has been self-employed most of his life.

At the age of 20, he was elected to the county legislature, where he has served for 23 years, part of that time as chairman and CEO of Niagara County, New York.

Lee's background is in small business and entrepreneurship. He served for a while as director of the small business program of Medaille

College in Buffalo. He spent many years as a business consultant, writing literally hundreds of reports on new business opportunities. He focused in particular on in-home, part-time small businesses.

"I saw it all," says Lee. "Everything from 'How to Have a Garage Sale' to 'How to Make Money Raising Hedgehogs.' And I wrote analyzes of many multi-level marketing programs, too. But I never saw anything that got me personally excited—until now.

"I was sitting in my home office one day leafing through *Success Magazine,* and an article about Betty Miles caught my eye. So I called directory assistance and tracked her down. She told me about the program, sent me some information and I decided to get involved."

When Lee called me, he didn't need a job. He was successfully self-employed and doing very well. But this opportunity was too good to pass up.

"This program is so powerful it has changed my focus," says Lee. "I have never lost a minute over anything, but I am beginning to lose sleep now. Not because of stress, but because my mind can't keep up with the tremendous potential of this business."

One thing that Lee, along with many other business owners, finds exciting about the new generation of network marketing is that many of the new companies no longer require the representatives to handle or distribute the products themselves.

Lee says: "I've never been impressed or involved with network marketing before, because they all handled products. It was a pain in the neck, because you were doing the grunt work for the company—accounting, inventory, collection. With most companies, it was more trouble than it's worth."

However, the new generation of network marketing companies offer many different programs.

That's one reason why former business owners—and even people who have tried network and multi-level marketing in the past—are reconsidering.

"When I talk with business

other business owners (I've owned my own business for more than 20 years) I know how to get their attention," says Lee. "I start telling them about a business with no employees, no offices, no overhead costs. I tell them that they don't have to make anything or collect money or make deliveries or hire an accountant. To them, it sounds like Heaven."

But network marketing doesn't just appeal to people with business backgrounds.

"When I first approached my parents, it was only as customers, not reps. I never asked them aboard, but they went to a presentation, and my father signed up.

"He's 75, and he just called me to get some more brochures."

Lee goes on: "Network marketing will allow the average person to finally get a piece of the pie. The dam has burst. It's not business as usual anymore. Network marketing will be there to allow people to enjoy and participate in the profits."

chapter six

"How to..."

Proven techniques that will make you a winner (Plus some tricks of the trade!)

Tips and hints on selling

Selling is stressful, yet rewarding. Being positive and enthusiastic is crucial to being a success. Preparing to sell is a skill that I have been constantly developing and improving for years. The following is a list of tips that have worked for me, and which I trust will help you, too. Practicing these procedures will prepare you mentally and physically for the wonderful world of sales.

1) Prepare for the day spiritually.

It is absolutely critical for me to get my mind focused, to remember the correct priority for the things in my life—God first, family second, business third. All the other priorities vary in position from day to day. But these three always remain the same. This quiet time, early in the day, prepares me for life's challenge in every endeavor I may attempt.

2) Prepare for the day physically.

It is very important to begin the day with exercise. I have tried many different activities from running, to treadmills, to TV aerobics. Sometimes I have only enough time to go up and down my stairs five times, but I have had great success using the physical aspects of yoga. Twenty minutes of slow bending and stretching movements, followed by several minutes of deep breathing exercises, leave me energized and refreshed rather than exhausted and sweaty. You need to find what works best for you, but be sure to prepare yourself physically every day. Take vitamins and/or supplements to ward off illness and provide extra energy.

3) Prepare for the day mentally.

Do not read the newspaper early in the morning if you want to meet the day in a positive frame of mind. Most daily news is filled with negativity which is neither uplifting nor inspiring. If you must be informed, try reading in the late afternoon when the news won't impact your business for the day. Instead, I begin each day by pretending I just found my new business. What would I do if I were just beginning to look for people to join me in this venture? I'd start with a list. Suddenly, I'm making a list of new people to talk to, and it's amazing how easy it is to think of new people, no matter now many times you've done it before. Select a positive thought or admonition to insert into your idle moments, those few seconds during the day when your mind is in neutral. Sometimes, I use the same thought for a week or two; sometimes, for an entire month, but usually I change this on a daily basis. This admonition can be spiritual, ("God loves me!" or "God is awesome!" or "Thank you, God.") or it can be motivating, ("Yes, I can!" or "Attitude determines altitude!" or "Go for it!") or even instructional ("I am lucky!" or "Keep it simple!" or "Plan your work, work your plan!").

4) Listen to motivational tapes in your car.

If you leave your home to go to an office, take some motivational tapes and listen to them as you drive. This not only improves your attitude and prepares you to sell, but it can have a positive effect on your blood pressure if you happen to live in a congested area with bumper-to-bumper traffic on the way to work. Foreign-language tapes or a favorite "how-to" tape might also be suitable, but be sure to save your final few minutes on the road for your favorite motivational speaker so that you enter your working environment prepared to uplift others who may not have had the relaxing and inspiring morning preparation that you have had. Be sure to greet everyone warmly, but not too enthusiastically. If they aren't a "morning person," too much enthusiasm may not be welcomed but genuine warmth will usually make anyone respond positively.

5) Begin your day with your most difficult tasks.

Once you get to your office or desk, open up your calendar to the list you prepared yesterday and start your hardest projects first. Getting those out of the way makes the rest of the day go smoother.

However, if you are working for someone else, and doing network marketing part-time, never steal time from your employer to do this business. Fit in time at lunch (bring a sandwich) or at break time. It is most important to set aside quality time to really focus. If you own the business, I still recommend that you keep the two businesses completely separate, but it will be much easier for you to develop your networking business if your hours are more flexible.

Overcoming telephone angst (or fear of the phone)

It is amazing to me how many people, who spend all day on the telephone, still have "telephone terror" when it comes to selling over the phone. Some people call it "call reluctance" or "telephone angst," but it is a definite problem when it relates to prospecting.

You see, the telephone is a machine of efficiency. Think of how many more people you can talk to in an hour on the phone, versus going to their homes or businesses. If you're in a business that depends on volume (and network marketing certainly does) you need to be able to effectively use the phone. If you can't, you may be a victim of "telephone angst."

What are the symptoms? Well, the phone seems to get heavier as you try to make sales calls. You can't seem to find a pencil, and when you do, it desperately needs to be sharpened three or four times. During call time, you always get very thirsty, or need to rush off to the washroom frequently.

Once the pencils are sharpened and your coffee cup is cleaned and filled, you look at your watch and it's LUNCHTIME! And everyone knows you can't make calls at lunchtime.

You can see how "telephone angst" can hurt your business. Every call you don't make is a check you didn't collect, a rep you didn't sign up and a downline you didn't start. Unless you want to spend your life working for someone else, you've got to put that telephone to work for you!

Here are a few practical tips on beating "telephone angst:"

1) Clean off your desk before you begin setting telephone appointments.

If you don't, you will find yourself thinking about many other subjects, and it is important to stay focused. No doodling or reading. The prospect deserves your full attention!

2) Write down exactly what you plan to say to the person you will be calling.

If you plan to ask a question, be sure you write down your anticipated response to both affirmative and negative answers. Your prospects won't always get their part of the script right, but if you have written down your important points, you will be able to continue without getting totally lost.

3) Always limit your time on the phone.

Your need to discipline yourself regarding the time you spend on the phone. Get a three-minute egg timer, and place it beside the phone. Remember, the person who is asking the questions is the one in control. If you allow your prospect to ask the questions, you have relinquished control of the conversation, and that usually occurs when you continue the call too long.

4) Even though you're on the phone, smile while you are talking, and stand when asking for an appointment.

They can't see you, but people can "hear" a smile. If the prospect believes you are smiling, he will automatically smile back, and be drawn into your enthusiasm. Also, standing up when you're asking for an appointment can generate energy, and help you focus on getting an appointment.

Enthusiasm is contagious! If you do not feel enthusiastic, just pretend that you do for a few minutes, and you will soon become enthusiastic. I learned that one day when I visited a Dale Carnegie graduation at one of his motivational seminars. The entire class stood up and began to chant, "Act enthusiastic and you'll be enthusiastic!" They repeated this statement several times in a short, choppy rhythm, and soon I was mentally with them. Every time I feel less than enthusiastic about a telephone call or an appointment I repeat this phrase until my attitude changes.

5) Always begin your conversation by asking if this is a good time to call.

Being polite and considerate of your prospects' time is very important. If you are calling at a bad time they won't be concentrating on what you are saying and they will be busy thinking of a way to rush the conversation. If there is a conflict and they ask you to reschedule, they will feel indebted to you and more receptive to your ideas because of your consideration for them.

6) Ask a warm-up question.

Once you have established that you are calling at a convenient time, ask a friendly question such as "How's the family?" or "How's business?" or "How's the job going?" or "Played golf lately?" Then actually listen to their answers. Many times they will provide you with the perfect opening. If their business is slow or the job is "same old, same old," you can respond with, "I know what you mean—that's why I started looking for something new, and I think you're going to love this business opportunity I've found." (This is sometimes called the "Feel-Felt-Found" reply—"I know how you feel; I felt the same way, until I found...") People respond to empathy if they believe your feelings are sincere.

7) Never get drawn into explaining the opportunity over the telephone.

When prospects ask you directly, "What kind of business opportunity is this?" give them enough information to prevent them from thinking you are trying to be deceptive, but don't try to give them a business presentation over the phone. This rarely works. I always tell prospects my business is telecommunications, but I quickly add that this is something they need to see, the information can't be explained fully over the phone. I invite them to a meeting or set up an appointment for breakfast, lunch or just a convenient time when they can spare about 30 minutes.

8) Make three attempts to get the prospect to a meeting.

The meeting can be either a group presentation or a one-on-one conversation. If, after three attempts, you have been unable to set an appointment or meeting, tell the prospect that this business is not for everyone, and ask them to call if they change their mind. This is part of the sorting process. It is important to know when to say, "Next!"

It is also very important to realize that the prospect is not saying a permanent "no." In many cases, they just aren't ready yet! This may not be the right time for them to get involved in a business venture, or they may not understand the value of the business. Also, remember, if they come in when you have reached a higher level in the company they will produce more income for you because most network marketing programs pay higher commissions on advanced positions.

Why Network Marketing companies have meetings

There are many different types of meetings associated with network marketing. Here we are discussing the standard, company-recommended Business Presentation (BP), which is sometimes called an "Opportunity Meeting."

The size of the BP depends upon the size of the organization presenting it. Generally speaking, BPs tend to have a life cycle; they start out small (10 to 20 attendees) and grow until they reach as many as several hundred. The meetings grow as the individual organizations of the reps develop, then many of the reps will break off from the original meeting and start a new (10 to 20 attendees) meeting of their own. Remember: this is a business of duplication.

The purpose of a BP is to present accurate facts about your networking company and to encourage and motivate new representatives. In most cases, the individuals who sign up at BPs have already been through a presentation of the company program, sometimes at a two-on-one (a rep and the rep's sponsor) meeting or a one-on-one (an experienced rep) meeting. Most people actually sign up in a less formal setting than the BP.

However, the BP is essential to a network marketing company, and all representatives are encouraged to attend at least one per week. If a rep has had a good week, the meeting needs the rep; if the rep has had a bad week, the rep needs the meeting!

Enthusiasm and motivation are absolutely critical in the network marketing industry. BPs are one of the best methods of generating enthusiasm while motivating all of the representatives, both new and old.

The BP is also important because a new rep or prospective rep is exposed to the quality of the organization—many doctors, lawyers, business executives, professors and a wide variety of professional individuals are getting involved in network marketing.

Many non-professionals are also joining our ranks, but that, too, has a positive impact because people love a business that anyone is capable of doing. New reps and prospects know they will be able to do this, if all types of individuals are doing it. While the professionals add credibility, the non-professionals add probability. The BPs provide the melting pot!

Some BPs are held in community club houses, recreational centers, public libraries, country clubs, Chamber of Commerce meeting rooms, private schools, church meeting rooms—we even had one group that met in the parlor of a nursing home. Most of these places are donated or rented for a nominal charge.

Most BPs around the country are held in motels, hotels, or restaurants. The costs vary widely, usually depending on the size of the anticipated crowd. Most hotels and restaurants have some small rooms available for groups of less than twenty. Restaurants usually make the room available, free of charge, if the attendees are going through the buffet or ordering from the menu. Breakfast and lunch meetings are very effective, and they can serve a dual purpose: I have said before, you can get prospects to a meeting if you *feed* them. Naturally, the rep always pays for the prospect's meal.

Some larger meetings (50 and up) actually charge a small amount at the door to cover the cost of the room. My company restricts this fee to a maximum of $5. Guests are never charged—only the reps.

7:30 p.m. is the recommended time to have evening meetings. My company asks all reps to hold meetings at this standard time, and it is recommended that the meetings last no longer than 45 minutes. The actual scripted, company approved presentation, is approximately 20 minutes long, with time at the conclusion for the speaker and top marketers to mingle with the guests and reps, answering questions and offering credibility. Short, power-packed meetings will encourage participation.

The presentation: Getting the most out of a meeting

1) Once a prospect has agreed to attend a business meeting with you, make arrangements to pick him up.

If you arrange to meet your prospects at the meeting, many times you will be disappointed. It is so easy for a thousand excuses to arise to prevent them from getting to the meeting. Think about how many times you have done that. Did you feel guilty? No, because most of us are masters at making excuses. Even if a prospect really wants to learn about the business, he probably prefers to procrastinate. Don't give him the opportunity to be a no-show—go pick him up!

2) Treat him to coffee or dessert.

If it's impossible to pick him up, at least get him to come to a nearby restaurant for a cup of coffee or dessert before the meeting. Offering food, even little bits of it, seems to get a positive response from most people. People are reluctant to turn down an offer of hospitality.

3) Tailor the meeting to your guests.

Arrive at the meeting place at least 15 minutes early and be sure to introduce your guests to the speaker. Mention their profession or line of work, along with any outstanding attribute that might help the speaker adapt the presentation to make the prospects more receptive. If the prospects feel at ease, they are more likely to pay close attention and join. If they believe you care about them, they will be encouraged to join.

4) Act fascinated by the meeting and presentation.

Always pay close attention to the speaker, nod slightly at the positive statements and laugh at the jokes, even though you've heard them a hundred times. Remember, you control your emotions! "Act enthusiastic and you'll be enthusiastic!" Your prospects will watch and respond. Never ask questions during the presentation, and if your guests ask you one, quietly tell them you'll answer the question as soon as the speaker finishes.

NEVER look at your watch. If you do, you might cause a chain reaction and see the entire row begin to look at their watches and begin fidgeting. Nothing is more disconcerting to a speaker—it suddenly disrupts his concentration and usually makes him talk faster because he fears he is running over the time limit. When the speaker begins to close the meeting, he will usually attempt to get the audience to nod in agreement with the final comments about the desirability of the business opportunity being presented. Be sure to nod along with him, so that your guest will feel positive about the presentation.

Never give prospects literature, or newspaper articles prior to the meeting. Wait until the conclusion of the presentation; otherwise, they will read and possibly rattle the paper during the meeting.

5) Listen carefully to your guests.

At the close of the meeting remain seated and immediately turn to your guest or guests and say, "Now that you've seen the presentation, how do you see yourself fitting into this company? As a customer, a marketer or a trainer?" Use the titles used in the presentation. Then STOP TALKING! This is very important. You will have a tendency to keep talking because of your enthusiasm and your desire to share that enthusiasm with your guest. But you may not need to continue closing if the speaker has closed the sale for you.

If your guest begins to ask questions about the various positions available in your company, pull out the application for the highest position first. If the guest is uncomfortable with that position, you can always move down. If there are only two positions available, and the guest is uncomfortable with the first, "assume" that he is selecting the second one, and begin filling out the application by asking how he spells his last name. If he doesn't stop you, keep filing in the application. If he does stop you by asking a question, be prepared to overcome any objection by reviewing *chapter eight.*

Network marketing provides an opportunity for unlimited potential for anyone, regardless of age, race, sex or education. No sales experience is necessary, but it IS necessary to have a strong desire to succeed and the willingness to work hard. This is a sorting process. You don't want to talk people into becoming a network marketer; you want to present the opportunity clearly and find the people who are drawn to it. Even though all types of individuals are capable of doing this type of business, not all of them will be willing to pay the price to do it well. This is a relationship business for people who care about others. Because of this, I recommend that you learn all of the answers to the objections and make sure you answer the ones you feel are arising from lack of information rather than lack of interest. Do not oversell in order to get a person to join your business. Do not tell them you will do all of the work for them. If they are not willing to make a commitment, move on to the next prospect.

6) Sign your prospect up on the spot.

If your prospect is one who sees the benefits of your company and "jumps" at the opportunity to make a change in his life, fill out the forms, congratulate him and be prepared to give him all of the start-up materials your company provides. Never allow a new marketer to leave without the ability to start learning about the business or talking to other people about it. He will be the most excited during the first forty-eight hours, and it is very important for him to channel that enthusiasm into productive activity. If at all possible, spend some time teaching your new rep the basics of selling your product or service, and a simple procedure for recruiting new reps for his downline. Make sure he starts a list of all the people he knows—not just the ones he thinks will do this business. Make an appointment to get back with him at the earliest possible time. When you find a prospect on fire, fan the flame!

7) Make sure your new representative is trained as soon as possible.

Knowledge will give him or her self-confidence to go along with that fresh enthusiasm. If your company offers a training program, use it. If not, formulate your own until the company is ready. Here are some tips on training that might be helpful.

Cultivating the reps: Tips on successful training

1) Help keep your reps enthusiastic by training them as soon as possible.

Most network marketing companies offer several levels of training. As stated above, it is vital for you to get your new reps trained as soon as possible. The initial enthusiasm in this kind of marketing will dissipate quickly without self-confidence. Self-confidence will be enhanced with knowledge of the product or service, as well as the basic steps required to obtain new recruits and customers. Early rejection in network marketing can be especially damaging to a person who has never been involved in sales. Training is important for product information, for motivation, and for sponsor and rep bonding. New reps need to know that they are in business for themselves, but not by themselves. They need to experience the team effort so they will feel comfortable seeking your assistance.

2) Make sure the initial training class is small.

Some network marketing companies provide large training

classes of 100 or more reps. This can be quite effective for advanced training, but the initial training that a representative receives is more effective if done in a class of 10 or less. This gives the rep the motivation of interaction with fellow representatives, while at the same time, providing the personal touch, which is very important for new representatives. They need to feel that they can ask all the questions they have and get individualized responses. This is also the perfect time to build their self-confidence, and give them the information necessary to successfully begin their business.

3) Conduct the training in a professional location and manner.

The location and atmosphere of the training class can be very important in conveying a professional image of the company and the business. It is important for reps to feel they are starting a business, rather than dabbling in a hobby. They need a desk and/or table to write on, note-taking materials and a workbook. If the workbook is not provided with their start-up materials, make sure you have one for them to purchase. Do not give away materials if you have to purchase them, although it is helpful to provide group purchasing, if a discount is available. Remember, you want to teach your reps that this is a business of duplication. You don't want them to think they will have to spend a great deal of money on supplies. If everyone spends a little, then no one will have to spend a lot.

4) Outline the agenda and stick to it.

At the beginning of the training class give out an outline of the training agenda and strictly adhere to the schedule. Start on time and finish on time. Begin the session by introducing yourself as the instructor, then allow the trainees to tell how long they have been in the business, who their sponsors are and why they decided to do network marketing. Many of the goals and dreams will act as motivation for the other participants. They will also help the group bond together, and this can be very beneficial in the future.

5) Help your new rep find his first recruit.

Once your new rep has been trained, it is critical that you help him find his first recruit. Remember, that's what networking is all about. No one is in this alone. Help him sign up his first customer. This will energize you as well as your rep, and the sharing and caring will change the work into fun. The sooner you help your rep feel the excitement of that first paycheck, the greater the chance he will be one of your winners!

Closing

What is closing? Closing is simply asking someone to buy. It is the process of "closing out" the demonstration or explanation stage of the sale and moving into the negotiation stage. It is going from, "Would you like to join our company?" to "At which level would you prefer to come in?"

The most important part of closing is to just do it! In marketing activities, 73% of the presenters never ask for the check. If you simply ask your prospect to fill out the application and give you a check, you are way ahead of three-fourths of the people in sales. The meeting itself may have closed your prospect. You won't know until you ask. So, at the end of the meeting, turn to them and say, "Now that you've seen the presentation, how do you see yourself fitting into this company?" Give them a choice of the various positions and wait for their response. The ones who are sold will give you an answer, and you should immediately begin filling out the forms. For the others, be prepared to overcome their objections by using the material in *chapter eight.* If you are the speaker, go around the room at the end of the meeting and assist in closing. If you have a guest, take care of them first, then see if you can help others. If you are not the speaker, ask for help from your upline, or any upline member that might be attending the meeting. You only ask for their assistance if you need information you have not learned yet, or if you need help in substantiating the credibility of the company.

Inviting people to a business presentation is one of the most difficult assignments for new representatives. Usually they do not have enough confidence in their knowledge of the business to comfortably share the information with others. Training should reinforce the fact that it is very important to limit the amount of information they share, before a full presentation can be made. Most companies have a standard presentation that has been reviewed by their legal department to make sure it complies with the various network marketing rules and regulations which vary from state to state. Therefore, it is extremely important in this industry, to adhere to the company-approved script when doing a presentation.

So, as a new representative, you don't need to know everything about the company. I've said before that we are in the business of helping each other, and these training meetings prove exactly that. A representative can immediately start expanding his downline (and his income) by inviting prospects to meetings conducted by those who are experienced in the business.

Closing is the most difficult part of the sales process because it is so forthright. Most salespeople never get this far. They talk about the product or service, they give explicit details about the company and the marketing plan, but they hesitate to come right out and ask for a check. They can overcome all the objections, they can answer any of the questions about the business, but they freeze when it comes to that final moment. But that final moment—the close—makes all the difference. Reps must learn to ask for the check. Just do it!

chapter seven

The three keys to success in Network Marketing

(And in life!)

It seems that we spend most of our time making life harder than it has to be. For example, listen to your friends who are always talking about "trying to lose weight." These are the ones who can give you the calorie count on every vegetable, and tell you the best time of day for your body to burn fat.

Meanwhile, we all know how to lose weight: Eat less and do more.

It's that simple. Not always EASY, but simple.

The same with making money. There is no magic to network marketing. The concept is very easy to understand. The potential is there for anyone to make a great deal of money in a relatively short time.

So, why isn't everyone in America getting rich? Because it takes more than knowing how to make money. You have to be willing to DO it.

That means stating your purpose, setting a high goal, committing whole-heartedly to achieving it and creating within yourself a burning desire to succeed. Once you have mastered these techniques, everything you desire becomes possible. Nothing is guaranteed, and we all fail from time to time. But if you stick to it, you'll have more than you ever dreamed.

Here's how:

Setting goals

In network marketing, as in any other type of business, establishing goals is important. There are three steps necessary in setting and attaining goals. They are:

1) State purpose

(This is the "why?" question)

Goals are important, but in order for a goal to gain momentum of any magnitude, it must have depth. It must be directed, linked to an overall purpose. The why in our lives is much more important than the "what," the "how," the "when" or the "where." Many of the difficulties we face in life from depression to drug addiction are the result of a void of purpose. We all want our lives to have "meaning," and sometimes the search for this meaning causes great emotional stress because without meaning or purpose, it is difficult to cope with everyday trials and tribulations.

It is not surprising that purpose is usually spiritual. It is too significant to be physical or emotional. It is the axle upon which the wheel turns; it is the center of the solar system; it is the very center of a human being's existence. The lack of purpose, or the lack of understanding of one's specific purpose, can result in confusion, disillusionment, frustration and depression. Lack of purpose gives a person a feeling of intellectual vertigo, a deep sense of loss, a hunger and thirsting that can't be satisfied by physical food or drink. When we feel that life is passing us by, that we don't know exactly what we're supposed to be doing, it's simply a subconscious awareness that we don't have a specific purpose. And if it isn't specific, it is not the overriding purpose of our lives. When we have a purpose, we know what it is. If we feel vague about it, we need to work on it.

Purpose is not synonymous with a burning desire. Purpose is the big picture that is fueled by the burning desire. Walt Disney's purpose was to make people happy. Disneyland was one of his burning desires. If we don't know what our life purpose is, we become more and more frustrated until we figure it out. We need to dig deep within to discover this very meaningful aspect of our personality, and once we have it, many things in life will suddenly fall into place—very much like the pieces of a puzzle. My purpose is to help people have hope. I believe network marketing is the perfect way for me to accomplish this purpose.

2) *Set goals*

(The "what?" question)

In 1953, Yale University took a survey of their senior class. The graduates were asked how many of them had formulated goals for their future. They all raised their hands. Then, they were asked how many had written down their goals and given them a deadline. Only three percent had done so. 20 years later when the alumni returned to the university for a class reunion, another survey was conducted. To everyone's amazement, 95 percent of all the earned income in the class had come from that three percent.

To be honest, I'm not so surprised. Until a goal is written down, given a deadline and looked at every day, it is merely a wish or dream and has a very slim chance of materializing.

When I first began network marketing, I set a goal for myself and I wrote it in tiny numbers on a little piece of paper, which I taped to the back of my watch. Having my goal taped to my watch was even better than looking at it because it scratched my arm, ever so slightly, as a constant reminder.

I also found that the deadline was a critical part of my goal-setting. At first, I was tempted to extend the amount of time as the deadline approached. But soon, I discovered that it was very important to keep the original deadline until the time had expired. Unbelievable things seem to happen at the very last minute if you are truly dedicated to meeting your deadline. I can remember many occasions when, in the last few minutes before the deadline, some miraculous event would push me over the goal line. If I had extended the time limit, I wouldn't have tried quite as hard to make my goal a reality.

Some people never have a deadline. Haven't you heard someone say, or thought yourself, "I wish I were a millionaire," or "I wish I were rich!" but they don't say, "I want to be a millionaire by one year from today." Think how futile a football or basketball game would be without a time limit. Those guys would just keep playing all night long! How about a cake in the oven without a deadline? Wouldn't taste too good, would it? We need to learn to turn our hopes and dreams into goals with a deadline. That's the second step on the road to success.

3) Make a commitment

(The "How" question)

Once you have crystallized your goals, you must make a personal commitment to reach those goals.

Without commitment, goals and emotions can quickly fade. Are you determined? How badly do you want to make $50,000 per month? When I am conducting motivational seminars, I often read the following statistics about a famous figure in history:

1831—failed in business
1832—defeated for state legislature
1833—failed in business again
1835—sweetheart died
1836—had a nervous breakdown
1838—defeated for speaker
1840—defeated for elector
1843—defeated for Congress

1848—defeated for Congress again
1855—defeated for Senate
1856—defeated for vice-president
1858—defeated for Senate again

But in 1860, Abraham Lincoln was elected the 16th president of the Unites States.

Now that's determination. Lincoln would have made a fortune in network marketing.

This is why commitment is vital. Your network marketing business is a microcosm of the world. You will experience every emotion on the scale from elation to depression.

The only way to achieve your goals is to be totally committed for whatever time you dedicate to this business. You may not be able to work it full time. Most people begin network marketing businesses on a part-time basis, but whatever amount of time you are willing to commit, make sure it is a 100 percent commitment. You will find that a genuine commitment, even for a small amount of time, will produce unusual results, when compared with the amount of time necessary to make a living in a "normal" job. This commitment can help you with personal growth and self-development, and will even help you with your regular business.

• *Commit to learning everything about the product or service.*

The validity of the marketing rests on the value of the service. Learn the material! Attend meetings and learn how to give presentations. Make a tape of yourself giving the presentation and learn by watching.

• *Commit to using the product or service.*

You cannot be enthusiastic about selling something you do not believe in. The last four letters of enthusiasm mean, "I Am Sold Myself." If you use the product or service, you will have personal examples to relay to others. You will be able to personally endorse the product or service. The more you use the service, the more successful you will be in explaining the benefits to others.

• *Commit to purchasing inventory and sales aids.*

Always have enough sales materials on-hand to help three new reps get started in the business. If your company uses a video, purchase enough to give each new rep one of the tapes. Teach your new reps to purchase the same amount of materials you did so that no one person has to spend a lot of money.

• *Commit to treating your network marketing opportunity as a business.*

Get business cards as soon as possible. Those can usually be ordered from your company. Like franchising, companies using Network Marketing to distribute their products and services have rules and regulations that must be followed. Make sure you comply with any company regulations regarding use of the company logo. Your cards will legitimize what you are doing. Keep a separate checking account; this will make it easier to take advantage of tax deductions that are business related. Make a separate file for your business-related expenses. Many attorneys say that owning your own business is the last tax shelter.

• *Commit to giving your time.*

Set up a meeting with your sponsor, and make a time commitment they can hold you accountable for. Do not hesitate to ask for help, but don't let them become a crutch. Learn as quickly as possible to do the same for the people you sponsor. Don't use time from your present job, if you are a salaried employee. Taking time from your current employer will not make you feel good about your new business. You can only be committed 100% to one business at a time. Being honest in every aspect of your business life is critically important to your success, and to your peace of mind.

• *Commit to create a "burning desire."*

We do what we want to, not what we ought to. So, the most important element of fulfilling your commitments is to create a desire within your own heart to achieve your goal.

Consciously creating "burning desire" is really not that difficult (this is covered in detail in Chapter 9). You just ask yourself a simple question: "If money were no object, what would I want to have or to do?" Now, many people will say they aren't sure what they want, but that's because they believe these burning desires come from within and they're still waiting for their subconscious to let them know what their desires really are.

I don't believe it works that way at all. I believe burning desires are ignited from the outside by our conscious mind, and I honestly believe we can create a burning desire for anything we so choose. All of us wish for things, but we don't get these things because we don't really pursue them. We just think about them occasionally—even half-heartedly—almost as if we're afraid to allow ourselves "to get our hopes up."

And why are we afraid? First, because we don't want to be disappointed and, secondly, because deep down we don't think we deserve our dreams. We have a self-image problem.

To solve it, we must convince ourselves that we really do deserve it, and can have it, if we truly want it and are willing to pay the price!

It reminds me of the plaque that hung over one of my insurance friend's desk. It read: "THE HARDER I WORK, THE LUCKIER I GET!"

real-life stories

Sue Turner

I believe network marketing is helping Sue Turner fulfill her purpose in life. When I shared the podium with her a few weeks ago at a sales motivation seminar, I asked her how she found out about multi-level marketing. She laughed and said, "When I first started this business, it was an in-between thing that I planned to do until I found a 'real' job. I was scared to death. Every time I had to pick up the phone to talk to people, I got so nervous I didn't think that I would be able to do it."

That's hard for some people to believe when they meet her today, one of the most articulate and successful people in Mary Kay. How did she get started?

"I was flat broke, working at Kroger's grocery store when a lady came through my check-out with the most beautiful skin I had ever seen," Sue says. "And she wanted to do a make-over for ME! I was very tempted, but I didn't even have the money for the make-up, so I said no.

"Later, when I was pregnant and on maternity leave, I was approached again and decided to get involved."

Like many network marketers, Sue's goals were very small. "I just wanted to be able to stay home with my children. I didn't know if I would be able to make enough money, but I wanted the freedom to do things with my children. In the early years, I don't think most people even knew what I was doing, because I was able to do all the things the other moms did, and work my business part-time."

Soon, network marketing became a way of life. She began to discover some of the "pleasant surprises" of sharing the network marketing opportunity.

"When I helped women look better, I realized that I was starting a chain reaction. I would affect not only the woman by making her feel better about herself, but I would make her children and husband and all of the people she came in contact with feel better, too. When she felt better about herself, it affected how she treated others," Sue told me excitedly. "It really became so much more for me than the dollars I made. I began to get paychecks of the heart. And that was what was so special about this business." However, as a single business woman, the paychecks bought Sue's dream home last year.

And the unforeseen benefits weren't just for her customers and consultants, either.

"I also realize now, looking back, that I was able to grow up emotionally with this business. I could focus on other people, I became less self-centered and more people-oriented. The more I began to care for others, the more self-respect I gained along the way.

"And this business has been awesome for my children. It has helped me to teach them to be independent. I have instilled in my children all of the attributes that I longed for them."

Today, with a three-year-old grandchild, Sue is as excited as ever about the opportunities in network marketing.

"In the last five years, I

have tripled my income and still have kept balance in my life. I have priorities, and I have been able to maintain those priorities: faith, family and career, and that is what is so wonderful about this kind of work. I have two assistants who help me and I call it work, but work is only work if you would rather be doing something else. For me it's a pleasure.

"I enjoy working with people, being a self-starter, and I enjoy having the freedom of an office in my home. In fact, I have two offices: One with my 'neat' desk, where I interview people, and one with my 'messy desk,' where I actually get things done."

While the "neat desk/messy desk" system may not work for you, Sue does have some valuable insights for people interested in joining the network marketing industry:

"If I had it to do over again, I would concentrate more on staying away from negative people," Sue confesses. "Also, people need to think about their goals, what they truly desire to accomplish. They need to know their purpose. My purpose is maintaining balance in my life, while helping others. The 'how-to' will come if you just know the 'why'. Knowing your purpose helps you compare the costs of your sacrifices. If you don't know your purpose, then the price is always too high. If your purpose is clear, the price is never too high."

I am so excited about getting to know Sue. When I look at her I see what so many people in America long for: A happy family, a hopeful future, and a life full of unseen opportunities and pleasant surprises.

Sue knows her purpose. Do you know yours? That's the first step on the road to success.

real-life stories

John Jones

I was on a program at Lincoln Center recently with John Jones, one of the most goal-oriented people I've ever met, and one of the most inspiring and motivating people in network marketing.

John is one of those unique people who can look ahead and see the "big picture." For example, after finishing his pre-Med degree, he realized that business savvy, not book work, was the key to success. So he went to work with a national company that offered management training.

"After a while," John tells the story, "I started studying shifts in the economy. I realized that the 1980's was going to bring an explosion in the telecommunications industry. So I left a safe job to go to work for AT&T, which was the leader in the industry at the time."

It was with AT&T that John made another astute observation: "The owners were creating the wealth, not the employees," says John. "If I didn't want to be part of that 99% of America, I needed to be creating value myself."

So John moved to yet another, more speculative, company: General Datacomm. "We actually manufactured the hardware and software used by the telecommunication companies. It was a booming, fast-moving business and before long I was working 18-hour days. And I might still be there today if it weren't for two events in my life."

The first was a visit to the doctor. "I was having tremendous chest pains, but I just ignored them," John confesses. "I didn't have time to be sick. My sister said I should see a doctor and I finally did. I was having 'stress attacks,' the doctor told me. He said I was all right today, but he wouldn't make any promises about tomorrow. That got my attention."

The second event also got John's attention. A longtime friend flew to New York from Atlanta, just to tell John about a business opportunity.

"I was really excited to see my friend, until he started talking network marketing. But a funny thing happened. He noticed I wasn't too enthusiastic, so he dropped it. I saw that he was going to take this opportunity away from me. That's when I focused on his message and saw what he was really offering. Sometimes you have to take the opportunity away for people to really see it."

The opportunity was in the field of telecommunications. John, once again demonstrating his foresight, flew to Dallas to check the company out for himself.

"I was familiar with Network Marketing, and I never had a strong positive or negative attitude about it. My mom had even been involved with a network company. What I saw in Dallas were people making 'New York' incomes. That impressed me."

John jumped into network marketing and never looked back.

"No one grows up wanting to work 18 hours a day. We start our careers working to achieve something, but we lose our vision. Eventually, we're just working to be working, just glad to have a job. That puts us in that 99%, people who are earning only as long as they are working, with little hope of achieving wealth or security or freedom.

"Network marketing allows you to work to accomplish your goals. I believe it is extremely important to set goals, both short and long term, as soon as you start your business, and I make sure my reps learn how to do that in the initial training.

"Being goal oriented gives you the possibility of achieving real wealth."

John is tremendously successful in network marketing and I believe the secret to his success is his emphasis on goal setting with his reps.

"When I approach people with my business, I tell them 'I don't want your time, I want your contacts. I want you to lean on me, and I will show your friends who are working 18 hours a day a way out.' All people really want is potential, opportunity. In traditional jobs, there's no potential for achievement. In network marketing, the potential is unlimited."

To help his downline achieve this potential John takes a mentoring approach to managing them.

"It's like a baby. When it's born, we teach it to crawl and walk. A good sponsor will treat a new rep the same way, will help him through the learning process, not just leave him to fend for himself.

"A good network marketer will also remember that his downline is watching how he does business. He will lead by example. A sponsor who is unmotivated and discouraged will often leave his downline the same way.

"It's really simple. The learning process in network marketing takes about a year. If your sponsor will help you survive the learning period, if you can stick with it, you'll probably do fine.

"That's why, unlike some others in this industry, my philosophy isn't 'sponsor, sponsor, sponsor,' signing up everyone I can. My approach is 'sponsor and teach.' This industry has too many 'sponsors' who have abandoned their rep 'children.' "

John's lesson is a good one. It reminds us why some people have failed at network marketing while their friends have succeeded in the very same company. Just as it is true that all network marketing companies are *not* created equal, downlines can vary dramatically in support and effectiveness.

If you're interested in network marketing, you should look at the success and motivation of the people in the downline you're considering.

"We teach our reps two lessons which we all need to re-learn again and again," says John. "The first is that all you can do in network marketing is plant seeds. Some people you reach will be like bamboo and shoot up quickly. Others will be redwoods, slow but steady. You can't control it. Like a farmer, all you can do is plant and water. The miracle of growth is out of your hands.

"Secondly, I keep reminding my reps that this business is like waves. Some days it seems everyone you talk to is signing up. Other days, you can't do anything right. That's when you're in the trough, and that's when inexperienced people tend to quit. My job is to keep them from making that mistake, to remind them that another wave is coming and they need to keep planting seeds."

John's final note: "It's amazing how hard it is for us to take failures, even small ones. You know, children fall down all the time, but they always get back up. It's not until we're adults that we learn to quit. Children don't know any better, and they usually end up getting where they're going."

real-life stories

John Pershing Smith

Not long ago, I was a guest motivational speaker at a network marketing training seminar in Atlanta, Georgia. John Pershing Smith was another speaker on the program. As I listened to his presentation I realized how fortunate I am to work with people who are absolutely committed to doing whatever it takes to be successful.

Later, my husband and I were fortunate enough to spend several hours with John and Bonnie Smith, and I asked John how he got involved in this dynamic industry. This is what he told us:

"My first experience in multi-level marketing came at the age of 22 when I started marketing some very expensive cookware. In 1964, a $395.00 set of cookware was a very hard sell, but, when I sold a set, I made $50.00. In a short period of time, I progressed to the next level where I was paid $75.00! Then, I sponsored a few individuals, who each made $50.00 a set, and I made a

$25.00 override—I couldn't believe it! Each time one of my folks made $100, I made $50. At that time, my full-time job at a department store was only paying $100 a week, and I was able to double my income in no time at all.

"However, to move to higher levels, I would have to purchase a large amount of inventory, and I just couldn't afford it, so I moved on, and tried several other opportunities over the years. I tried soap, encyclopedias, vitamins, cosmetics, diet shakes, and more, with limited success and always got stuck with excess inventory. However, my belief was still strong that network marketing was my real chance at personal and financial freedom.

"My first real success in a multi-level marketing program came years later when I joined a major 'buy term & invest the difference' life insurance operation. I spent ten years there, became a National Sales Director, built a sizable sales organization, and earned a significant amount of money.

"The problem with the insurance business was the complexity of it; new regulations and licensing made it difficult to recruit folks.

"In 1988, I went through a traumatic divorce, ending a 27-year marriage, and the devastation of bankruptcy. It was then the realization hit me—this company would not continue to pay me unless I was there all the time to run it!

"This was not my American Dream! Network marketing is supposed to build a residual income that will continue, even if you become disabled and can't be there to run your business.

"I began looking for a company with a simple marketing plan—a plan that paid true residual income, required no inventory, deliveries, or collections; yet offered a product used repetitively by almost everyone, without changing anyone's habits! A company with a successful track record and examples of representatives who were making money!

"In my search for this 'dream company,' I investigated 25 to 30 new deals—each brand new—each about to revolutionize the world. Almost all of these companies started out with limited funds, and are out of business today.

"I continued to believe that I would find the perfect company, match it with my abilities and my 'burning desire' to be somebody special, and fulfill my dream of total financial freedom.

"But, first, I needed someone to help me build this dream. After two years of lonely single life I ran an ad in the personal column of my newspaper, and God sent Bonnie Melinda Zane into my life. She was the only one who answered the ad, and we both knew immediately that we were meant to be! The similarities were absolutely eerie! It was as if we were separate parts of a magnet which came together and just 'clicked'.

"About four years later, an old friend of mine, Ronny Kirkland, called and told me about the company we are involved in today. It was my 'dream' company! It had every single aspect I had been looking for all my life!

"At the time, I was in a corporate executive salaried position in Jacksonville, Florida, as the senior vice-president of national marketing and training for a large insurance and telecommunications company. Bonnie was teaching IV Therapy to long term care nurses in nursing homes in North-East Florida. We were doing fine financially, but I believe you've got to be ready when your opportunity arrives; so three weeks later, I resigned and went full-time in this wonderful telecommunications networking company. I had total faith that it would work for us and it has done exactly that!

"Today, we reside just outside of Atlanta, Georgia. Bonnie has been able to retire, after 30 years as a registered nurse. We are now partners in every way.

"Bonnie and I have spent many years in corporate America, always having a boss dictate our every move. But today, after just 24 months with this incredible company, we are finally beginning to realize our 'American Dream' of being totally financially free. I have a little saying which I use with pride: 'In the last few years, God has smiled on me twice. First, he sent my Bonnie, and then, he sent Ronny with this network marketing dream.' "

John and Bonnie now have financial freedom because they have taken the necessary steps on the road to success. All three steps—stating your purpose, setting your goals, and making a commitment—are necessary before a person accomplishes a true goal or mission. Unless these steps are taken, a goal remains a wish or a dream.

chapter eight

The ten most common objections to Network Marketing

(And my ten favorite answers!)

Read the profiles of successful network marketers in this book and you will discover a common thread: They all said "No!" to network marketing! But eventually they overcame their objections, got answers to their questions and agreed—perhaps unenthusiastically—to attend a presentation or review the program. Today, earning incomes as high as $1,000,000 a month, they are all very glad they did!

Many of their stories begin with intelligent motivated people who had objections that their sponsors had to overcome. You are very likely to hear these same objections as you invite people to join your business, too. But if you do, you're just as likely to sign up another "superstar."

I have compiled some of the most common objections I hear from people I approach about network marketing, along with my favorite answers. You may hear yourself in some of these dialogues, many of which are based on actual conversations.

A Note to Network Marketers: Your goal is to answer all of the objections and arrive at a positive conclusion! Your preference, of course, is to sign up a happy and productive new representative. If that does not happen, the next best outcome is a reluctant decliner—a person who is not quite sure they made the right decision. He is someone you can come back to later, when you have demonstrated that the business really works. Never burn your bridges!

The ten most common objections:

1) I don't have time.
2) I don't know many people.
3) I need to check with my wife (or husband).
4) Is this selling?
5) This type of business is not for me.
6) Let me think about it.
7) Is this some pyramid scheme?
8) My business takes 100% of my efforts. I don't want to get unfocused.
9) I don't have the money.
10) Is this multi-level marketing?

Let me start by saying you can answer any of these objections with the "Feel-Felt-Found" response I mentioned in Chapter 6: "I know how you FEEL. I FELT the same way until I FOUND..." Empathy is a powerful tool!

If you did not personally experience the objection, you may use another member of the business as your example. Always be truthful. Establish credibility early in network marketing.

Here's a real-life example of how one representative I know misused the "3F" response:

Rep: Well, Tom, now that you've seen our presentation, how do you see yourself fitting into this business: as a marketer, a trainer or a customer?

Prospect: Sounds great, Fred, but I just got a promotion at work, and my wife's complaining now because she never sees me. I just don't know when I'd have the time.

Rep: I know exactly how you feel, Tom. I felt the same

way until I found that I could make as much doing this part-time as I was making full time.

Prospect: But I thought you started this right after you were laid off.

Rep: That's right, but what I meant—what I was trying to say—I can just imagine how I would fit this in, if I still had that job.

Prospect: Sure, Fred, but I think you've got a better imagination than I do. If I don't stay focused, I may get laid off myself.

Fred blew it! The 3F response works well if the empathy is genuine. The quickest way to lose total credibility is to misrepresent your "true" feelings. Fred had learned about empathizing with the prospect in training, but he applied it in the wrong way. He could have used it in the following manner:

Rep: Well, Tom, now that you've seen our presentation, how do you see yourself fitting into the company: as a marketer, a trainer or a customer?

Prospect: Sounds great, Fred, but I just got a promotion and my wife's complaining now because she never sees me. I just don't know when I'd have the time.

Rep: Tom, I know exactly how you feel. That's how my sponsor felt, too, until he found that he could do this business on the side in just a few hours per week. After a few months, his part-time income was as much as his full-time.

Prospect: That's amazing! What exactly would I have to do?

Fred has used empathy through a surrogate since he had not experienced the same situation himself. For every objection there will be some individual in your organization who has experienced a similar situation. Just make sure when you use the 3F response, you are completely honest.

Now, let's tackle that Top Ten List!

1) Question:***"I don't have time."***
Answer: ***"How much time do you think it takes?"***

Whatever amount of time the prospect gives you, divide it in half. Example: If they say, "It would probably take a couple hours a day, at least," then you say, "You could really do it in one hour a day." If they say, "I do not even have one hour a day," then you say, "You could do it in one hour a week."

You are trying to find out where they're coming from. Because you can actually do most network marketing plans any amount of time you choose, it's smart to get an idea of what they consider too much time. That's what's so nice about being in a flexible business. You must be sure to explain that their earnings will probably be in direct proportion to their efforts, so the amount of time they dedicate to this business will definitely be reflected in their monthly check or checks.

Here is the WRONG way to answer this objection:

Prospect: Bob, I really appreciate you thinking of me, but I just took on that PTA job, and the kids start tee-ball next week, and the choir at church is just beginning to practice for our pageant. This sounds great, but where could I fit it in?

Rep: Look, you don't even get paid for those things. You could make really big bucks doing this.

Prospect: Some things are more important than money, Bob. Rep: Mary, couldn't you just put some of that on the back burner for just a short time?

Prospect: My kids or my church?

Rep: OK, you're right, but this is telecommunications—the information superhighway. It's a once in a lifetime deal!

Prospect: So are my kids, Bob!

Bob hit all the wrong hot buttons for a busy, conscientious mother. He first tried to lure her with money, then he challenged her maternal instincts. Nothing could be more futile. He could have handled the same situation in a much different manner:

Prospect: Bob, I really appreciate you thinking of me, but I just took on that PTA job, and the kids start tee-ball next week, and the choir at church is just beginning to practice for our pageant. This sounds great, but where could I fit it in?

Rep: How much time do you think this takes?

Prospect: I don't know, but I don't even have an extra hour a day.

Rep: Mary, you could do this on a part-time basis a couple of hours a week, and make some extra income to start a college fund for those boys of yours.

Prospect: Are you sure that's all it would take?

Rep: Absolutely, you can do this any amount of time you choose as long as you give it 100% for that specific time. I'll help you and so will our whole group. This is a business of people helping people. You'll love it.

Prospect: Well, I guess I could try. I have been concerned about the college money, and there are a couple of people at church who need to do this, too.

Bob is now appealing to Mary's maternal instincts by giving her the opportunity to provide for her children. He is also appealing to her gregarious nature by offering group help to her.

The primary objective when a prospect says she has no time is to convince her that this business opportunity is flexible and will work even with a very limited amount of time because of the help of others.

2) Question: ***"I don't know many people."***
Answer: ***"In this business, we get paid to help others. I'll be with you every step of the way!"***

Many times people with this objection are merely shy and hesitant to talk to strangers. There is definitely a wrong way to deal with a shy prospect.

> *Prospect:* This looks like a great opportunity, Sue, but I just don't know very many people.
>
> *Rep:* You don't have to. One of my reps moved here from Maine and everyone in her organization was a total stranger.
>
> *Prospect:* Oh, I could never talk to strangers. I'm just not a people person.
>
> *Rep:* Don't be silly. Of course you can. I do it all the time.
>
> *Prospect:* That's because you are a people person, Sue! I just can't do it.

A better way to handle a shy person is as follows:

> *Prospect:* Gosh, Sue, I wish I were as outgoing as you are. I just don't know that many people, and I could never talk to strangers.
>
> *Rep:* You don't have to. We get paid to help others in this business. You've got me, and we'll have a great time doing this together.
>
> *Prospect:* Well, I do need the money, but I'm going to count on your help.

Sue is offering much more than a business opportunity. She's offering Ellen friendship and a way to build her self-esteem. Even though this business is hard work, it seems like fun when you do it with a good friend.

If a person who uses this objection is new to the area, a better reply would be as follows:

> *Prospect:* We just moved here a couple weeks ago and I don't even know my neighbors yet, Steve. I should probably wait until we get established.
>
> *Rep:* Timing is very important in network marketing,

John. I don't think you should put this off. One of our leading producers had just moved here when he started and he's built a tremendous business. And don't forget, you can sign up people back home.

Prospect: I do think my sister in New York City would be great at this.

That's one of the great pluses about this business. It's not necessary to know a lot of people personally. Many of our reps have had only one or two contacts and have developed very successful networks. Our training program teaches reps to build a strong business even with a limited number of personal contacts.

3) Question: ***"I have to check with my wife (or husband)."***
Answer: ***"That's fine, when can we all get together?"***

Never argue or try to get around this objection. If the couple normally makes financial decisions together you will have a very difficult time working with the new rep. He or she will usually have an unsupportive mate throwing cold water on everything they do. This objection needs to be avoided before the meeting.

When you invite a person to a business presentation or to a one-on-one meeting, always ask if they need to get their spouse's approval before making a financial commitment. This will save you the time and effort of having a second meeting before signing them up because you can make sure the spouse attends the initial presentation.

4) Question: ***"Is this selling?"***
Answer: ***"How do you feel about selling? Do you like it?"***

Remember we are trying to get inside the prospect's head. Never prejudge! Many people love to sell. I know because I'm one of them. If they say yes, then you say, "Great! You're going to love this business. It's the easiest selling I've ever seen." If they say no, you say, "Great! You're going to love this business. Introducing people to this company is just like telling them about a good movie or a terrific restaurant—you're sharing! The only difference is, the movie or restaurant owners won't send you any money for your word-of-mouth advertising. Our company will.

5) Question: ***"I want to think about it."***
Answer: ***"I can certainly appreciate that. It's not the speed of a decision that counts, but the accuracy of it, right? Just for my own information, what is it exactly that you want to think about? The company? The product?"***

You are asking this question to find out if they really want to think about it, or if they are just using that as an excuse. If they specify one of the areas you mentioned, go back through the information you gave them originally. If they say they have a concern about the company, go back over several points that substantiate the fact that this is a strong company.

Name several prominent individuals who have checked out the credibility of the company.

Show them any financial material you may have. Give them copies of any newspaper or magazine articles you have that discuss the positive aspects of this business.

If they want to think about the product or service, review the product literature and brochures with them and tell them your personal experience using this service. Name some well-known people or companies that are using the service, and if possible, give your prospect the name of a satisfied customer for them to call. People always like to have a reference whom they can call, even though most people will not bother to actually make the call. If your product or service is guaranteed, be sure to show them that in writing. If you or your upline have a teleconferencing system arrange for them to listen to or participate in a teleconference call so some of your upline can give you added support.

6) Question: ***"I don't think this type of business is really for me."***
Answer: ***"You know that really surprises me, since you work well with people, and I know you enjoy helping people. What part of the business concerns you?"***

Use the same answers as "Think About It" above.

7) Question: ***"Is this one of those pyramids?"***
Answer: ***"I can understand your concern."***

Do not get angry or defensive! I know many network marketing representatives love their company as much as I love mine, but there are misconceptions about what network marketing is.

Say to them: I was worried about the same thing until I checked this plan out. There is no similarity! Illegal pyramids are schemes and rarely have a decent product for sale. They promote the recruitment of players and generally have a high capital investment required to get involved. As you can see, this company is nothing like that. You can start at any level of investment you find comfortable, or even no investment at all.

We are simply using network marketing which is nothing more than an organized form of word of mouth advertising. Network marketing is a method of distribution, like retailing is a method of distribution.

If they still have concerns about network marketing, you may want to give them a copy of this book, or perhaps a copy of *Wave Three* by Richard Poe. Make sure you have highlighted the positive points. Mention the many prominent people who have extensively checked out network marketing. Also, ask your upline to talk to the prospect in order to establish the company's credibility.

8) Question: ***"I don't want to get unfocused: my current job takes 100% of my efforts."***

Answer: ***"How well are you doing with this job you are totally focused on? Is it providing all the income you need? Will it lead to financial freedom in the next five years?***

Ask them to try giving your network marketing business 100% of their efforts just one hour each day. When their income from this part-time business equals what they earn from their existing company or job, they'll reevaluate the situation. I guarantee it!

9) Question: ***"I don't have the money."***
Answer: ***"Suppose your car that's parked in front of my house right now won't start when you get ready to leave in a little while, and we call and find out that it's going to cost (insert the amount of money required to get started in the networking company) to get your car running. Would you just leave the car here? No, of course you wouldn't. You would find a way to get the money because you would have a need (an urgent need) to get the car to provide you with transportation. You have the same need for network marketing—for financial freedom—so you won't have to worry about an unreliable car!"***

Many times, this objection is merely an excuse for not making a decision. In most situations, the person can find a way to get the money to begin a network marketing opportunity. Most of these companies do not require any type of investment and it costs no more than a couple hundred dollars to purchase the supplies and training necessary to successfully begin the business. Your main objective in overcoming this objection is to help the prospect think of a way to get the money if it were truly necessary.

10) Question: ***"Is this multi-level marketing?"***
Answer: ***"How do you feel about multi-level marketing?"***

If they say they like it, say, "Great! Then you're really going to like this business."

If they say "no", they still haven't answered your question. You need to find out what it is they DON'T like. Is it the concept of networking they don't like, or do they actually believe it's a scam? Have they had a negative experience with a multi-level company in the past? This is the information you need, so keep asking questions! Don't try to convince or explain—just ask.

Then you'll know which questions to answer. If they think network marketing is an illegal pyramid, you can show them the appendix in this book which explains the law. That's easy.

But if they just don't like networking, if they've tried it once and ended up with a basement full of vitamins they couldn't sell, that's tougher. What I do is to simply explain how my company works, how different network marketing is today than it was five or ten years ago, and then I share the opportunity with them. "Doubting Thomases" may take longer to see the opportunity, but be patient, be positive and be persistent. If that doesn't work, say "Next!" and move on.

Closing versus persuading

This chapter has been about answering objections. But let's not forget that your objective is to get people signed up. It's easy to get excited about your business and talk people's ears off with information, but it may be information they don't need or want.

Your goal isn't just to give information; it's to get results. Answering objections is part of a more important task: Closing the sale. Remember to close after each objection by asking, "How do you see yourself fitting into our business? As a customer, a marketer or maybe a trainer?"

Then wait. Don't say anything else until they give you their answer. If they are still reluctant after closing three times, tell them you understand and would appreciate it if they would at least commit to making a decision over the next 48 hours. Tell them you are willing to accept a "yes" or a "no," but you really have trouble handling a maybe. This type of deadline will help both of you.

If they agree, wait two days and call them to get their decision. If they are going to be enthusiastically involved, they will probably call you before the time period expires. If you haven't heard from them in the 48-hour period, you will probably get a "no," so be prepared to accept it cheerfully.

Don't try to "hard sell" people to join network marketing. They need to have a desire to change their lives, to move out of their comfort zone, or they will have a difficult time making the necessary commitment. But don't forget to keep the door open for the future. As your business develops and expands, many things will change, and you can always go back later.

If the answer is "no," be cheerful, be brief, and think "Next"!

real-life stories

Bob Capes

Many people say they love to sell. I know because I'm one of them. If people say that, I reply, "Great! You're going to love this business. It's the easiest selling I've ever seen." That's the answer I gave Bob Capes, the best salesman I've ever known, when he said he got into sales out of necessity and has loved it ever since. He recalled asking himself, "So, do I sell cars, life insurance, ladies' shoes or real estate?"

With that question, Bob began a career track that would build a multi-million dollar real estate company—AND a thriving network marketing business.

It was 1968 and Bob was a successful manager for Southern Bell in South Carolina...too successful, it turned out:

"I managed one of Southern Bell's long distance information departments. Back then, every long distance call had to go through an operator. I had 700 operators in my division, all of them women. It's hard to imagine without today's technology, but there were huge rooms of women, all at switchboards, handling each long distance call. On Christmas and Mother's Day, it was a madhouse.

"After eight years they wanted to move me to Miami, Florida. Well, I had a family and a home, and I didn't want to leave South Carolina. So I left Southern Bell instead, and I started looking for a job where I wouldn't be expected to relocate my family on the whim of an employer. I wanted more control over my life."

"What kind of business could a young professional in the 1960's go into outside of a corporate bureaucracy?

"If it were today, I would have gone into network marketing, absolutely. But at the time I said 'Well, I could either sell cars, life insurance, ladies' shoes or real estate. I chose real estate.' "

A wise decision, as it turns out. Bob Capes Realty is one of the largest commercial real estate firms in the state. Typically, however, Bob began with modest goals: "Honestly, all I ever wanted was an agency with 10 agents, and I planned to continue selling, too."

How many agents does he have today? "About 250," he says with a laugh.

So, with a successful, multimillion dollar real estate business, why did Bob get involved in network marketing?

"With a company like mine, at any given moment you're millions of dollars in debt *on properties you own* and you've got hundreds of agents—each one a potential lawsuit. It's rewarding, but it's very hard work," says Bob.

"In just 27 months, I'm almost making as much with my network marketing business as I am with my thirty-year-old real estate company."

Bob also disputes the notion that successful people aren't interested in network marketing.

"When I first started prospecting for this telephone company, I thought only of people who were in great need. I knew network marketing was a way for them to change their lives.

"They were the first people I called. It was a big mistake.

"You see, there is a reason

why some people have never made any money. They aren't motivated to financial success, or they aren't willing to do the work. When I sign people up today—both in my real estate business or in my network marketing business—I look for people who have succeeded before. Maybe it's something not related to business, like getting a scholarship through college, or making Eagle Scout or having a successful paper route as a kid, whatever. What's important is that they are motivated by accomplishments, they want to succeed."

Today, Bob reaches out to successful people with professional backgrounds. As a result, his downline is growing rapidly, along with his income. His philosophy for success in network marketing is simple:

"Work with the willing. I don't spend a lot of time trying to convince people to get involved.

"I show them the opportunity, and they either see it or they don't.

"Once they're in my downline, I try to help them early on, encourage them to go to meetings, to set goals and stick to them. If one of my reps calls and asks me to go to a meeting, I'll drive all the way across the state. But if they aren't motivated, if they stop calling, eventually I have to move on."

With thirty years of sales experience, Bob knows what to look for in a rep: "The people who tend to fail in this business are the ones who come in and right away start telling me about their MBA," laughs Bob. "This business is hard work, and it takes long hours and dedication to have tremendous success. People who tell me right off the bat they don't want to work nights or weekends, I usually assume they aren't going to go all the way."

The sign of a good rep? "They've got to be hungry for something—money, position, maybe they want to 'be somebody.' I've had some success because I'm never satisfied. I always want to see how much more there is to achieve," Bob says.

"I tell people, 'Network marketing will give you the opportunity, the vehicle, the means to achieve great wealth and freedom. But it can't give you the desire. You've got to find that within yourself.'"

Bob is the consummate salesman.

real-life stories

Steve Hammond

What if people say they don't like selling? That's what Steve Hammond said. I say, "Great! You're going to love this business."

Introducing people to this company is just like telling them about a good movie or a terrific restaurant—you're sharing! The only difference is, the movie or restaurant owners won't send you any money for your word-of-mouth advertising. Our company will.

When I asked Steve why he didn't like selling, he said, "I was raised with the belief that few things in life were more important than getting a good education. Knowledge for knowledge's sake was admirable and teaching was the most revered of professions. Perhaps then it was not surprising that my plans for medical school were rerouted, and through some unusual circumstances I found myself in front of a classroom of high school students even before I graduated from college. It was where I was supposed to be.

"I loved the interaction with students and guiding their boundless optimism and potential.

"But my path did not have classroom teaching in it for long. Shortly after I started this classroom odyssey I was asked to become the principal of a nearby elementary school. Not long after that I was appointed Superintendent of Schools of our system, the position I hold today. Like the circumstances that initially guided me into the classroom, I was led into school administration. I have enjoyed it all! Schooling, with all its joys and challenges, has been a marvelous blessing in my life.

"Like the old country song goes, 'If I had to do it all over, I'd do it all over again.' I have not a single regret. But I do have one great concern. Retirement.

"My pension plan depends on Social Security to cover my wife's and my needs upon retirement. Now that's a scary proposition! I invite each of you to find out what your expected Social Security benefits will be. In the best of circumstances, it isn't pretty. If Social Security remained intact and provided benefits at current levels, it would only provide a very meager subsidy. But many people have doubts that Social Security will even be around much longer. Perhaps you have similar concerns. I do.

"Still, when an engineer friend of mine invited me to take a look at a network marketing company, I quickly refused. Very graciously, I thanked him, but insisted that I didn't have the time or the inclination to devote to such an enterprise. 'This is the busiest phase of my career,' I explained to Jerry, 'and besides,' I said, 'I'm really not a salesperson.' I insisted; he persisted until I saw a presentation. I am so glad he did! Had he not, I might not have seen what is proving to be the solution to my retirement concerns.

"I discovered that I did not have to be a salesperson to be successful and I could find another few hours a week to pursue this business. I am not alone. Most of the people in my business are white collar workers who see the financial opportunity looming before them—savvy professionals who have reprioritized some of their activities and found time to created a more secure life for themselves. I am joined by doctors, lawyers, bankers, teachers, accountants, insurance executives and financial planners, stock brokers, retired executives, directors of not-for-profit corporations and the list goes on and on. It is a joy to work with these highly skilled persons and to be in a position to help them reach their financial goals.

"The American economy is simply not keeping up with the needs of the American people. It is affecting people across all socio-economic strata and causing them to look for financial opportunities today where they wouldn't have just a few years ago. Necessity is the mother of invention.

"What I am thrilled about with the discounted long distance company that I have selected is that nearly anyone can be successful in the business. So, not only do I have professionals in my business, I also have plenty of hard working class people who are doing exceptionally well. Tamara Van Noord in Paris, Texas works hard at cleaning apartments. Tamara joined our company and in the first few weeks signed up over 30 managing representatives! She won't be cleaning apartments for very long! The fact that this company can appeal to so many people in so many walks of life is its greatest strength.

"Everyone can make money, big money.

"If you had asked me eighteen months ago, if I would be working in a network marketing company, I might have simply laughed and said, 'No, I don't think so.' Today, not only am I working in it, I am thoroughly enjoying it! Giving presentations is like lecturing in the classroom. That's always been a joy. And I'm working with some of the most motivated, energetic people I've ever known. In a word, I'm teaching again and I love it.

"I have been very lucky throughout my life. In high school and college, I enjoyed pleasing successes academically and athletically. I have a wonderful career which is energizing and meaningful. Renae, my wife who is my high school sweetheart, and I have two of the greatest children in the world, Jeremy and Maggie. I'm fortunate. And I am fortunate for having this exceptional opportunity in this fabulous network marketing company which is changing the financial landscape of my life! However, I don't tend to call these things 'luck' or 'circumstance' anymore. I'm more apt to call it grace. Grace happens and it can happen to you."

real-life stories

Dr. Joe Rubino

Dr. Joe Rubino had a million-dollar dentistry practice and a solid reputation in his industry.

What was his reaction when first approached about network marketing?

"Absolutely not! It left a bad taste in my mouth," quips this successful dentist.

He had seen an ad in a dental trade journal for a non-alcohol mouth rinse. But when he found out it was a network marketing company, "I didn't want to leave my phone number.

"But they gave me some samples and a no-risk trial offer. It turned out that the product worked very well. That's when I began to think about getting in the business. It was a good product, one I knew my fellow dentists would use. But while I had confidence in the product, I was skeptical about the marketing program. So I just asked my good friends, who were dentists, to give it a try."

The result was a new network marketing company, a sister to Oxyfresh Worldwide, called the Dental Buying Network. Joe's company put dental products into waiting rooms, giving dentists an additional way to make money—a classic example of the adage, "find a need and fill it."

"When we started putting together the business we asked ourselves; 'What would be the one thing that would get dental professionals to look at what we're offering?' The answer was easy: money. So we set about looking for a way to cut 20% off the price of dental supplies and expand our markets. It worked. We were 20% below catalogue prices with a full range of dental supplies and services."

So that's how you get people to buy your products. How do you get them to SELL them?

"We would lead with the product, which we knew was excellent, then we would approach customers about the marketing program," says Joe. "We had five or six different programs for dentists, one of which was the 'Colleague Referral Program.' We were so successful that the Dental Buying Network and Oxyfresh formed a partnership."

Joe explains how he was able to get successful dentists involved with network marketing:

"We asked dentists 'How much would you work if you didn't have to? What kind of income would they need to have that freedom?' Then, we would follow by asking, 'Would you look at a marketing plan which would allow you to practice dentistry, not out of need, but out of choice?' The response was very positive."

That's putting in mildly. Joe Rubino signed up 1,000 reps in less than 3 months!

"To start a successful network marketing company, we had to address two issues: the integrity of the company, and the integrity of the network marketing industry. When I got into this business, I had classmates from dental school ask me 'Why are you doing that pyramid stuff—isn't your practice doing well?' When I told them that I had a million dollars and I was still getting into network marketing, that helped clear up some of those credibility issues.

"The most important element to success in network marketing is to have good reps working with you. And the good news is that people can LEARN to be good at network marketing, they don't have to be born good reps. You can help people develop the skills they need—listening, persistence, organization, charisma—people can actually develop the qualities of charismatic people."

Joe sees a bright future for network marketing today.

real-life stories

Jimmy Dick

Jimmy Dick, a successful broker dealer, said "no" to network marketing more times than anybody I know. When I first met Jimmy a year ago, I knew immediately that he was the kind of guy who could be successful at anything he tried. I told him I was writing a book and would love to ask him a few questions. He agreed and the conversation went something like this:

"Jimmy, why would a white collar professional whose six-figure annual income ranks in the top 2% of all wage earners in America get involved with network marketing?"

"That's a very good question," he replied. "I have to admit there is some stigma attached to multi-level marketing. Most professional people see such activity as something beneath them; and consequently, are reluctant to get involved. These were once my sentiments, and for twenty years, I resisted many attempts by friends and associates to get me involved in network marketing.

"I refused for several reasons. First, every business I had seen that was legal and reputable, required me to stock and pass inventory to a consumer population, either directly or through a downline. That's time consuming and labor intensive, and when I analyzed the financial return on my efforts, I was never quite convinced that it was worth it. In other words, I could do as well or better financially by continuing my current consulting activities."

At 52, Jimmy had quite a varied background. He had a degree in social work, had served as Director of Consultation & Education at the Mental Health Center in Sumter, South Carolina, and had started his own pension administration and investment advisory firm in the early eighties. As president and owner of Dick & Associates, he designed and installed qualified and non-qualified pension plans, group medical plans, and insurance programs. He also gave investment advice as a principal in a broker dealer firm.

Jimmy continued, "Now, don't get me wrong, even though I had avoided network marketing, I had always been fascinated by the concept of numbers growing exponentially; and I firmly believe that, given the right product and the right marketing design, the potential is virtually unlimited.

"When a friend contacted me in February, 1994, about network marketing for a long distance telecommunications company, I knew it had finally happened. The perfect product had been paired with the most powerful and the most cost-effective marketing strategy known to mankind! I began playing with the numbers, and even with the most conservative assumptions, the results were unbelievable! I was hooked!"

I talked with Jimmy about the incredible success he and his wife, Kathy, had experienced in the brief two year period they had been working the telecommunication business. In eight months they had earned enough to close down the consulting firm that had netted them a six figure income for many years. In fact, they were making almost that much monthly in the new business. When I asked Jimmy the secret to his success, he smiled and began to tell me the following little story:

"Betty, I really can't explain what's happening, but I do have a theory. I was invited to be the guest speaker for a large group a few weeks ago. I glanced at the program, as I waited to be introduced, and was surprised to see, 'Success' listed as my topic for the evening.

"I was totally unprepared to deliver a speech on that subject, so I anxiously looked around, spied a man behind me with a spiral notebook, and asked him for a piece of paper. As he tore it out, I noticed a little boy about five, smiling at me. His name tag said, JOSH. I asked Josh if he could draw a picture of a horse for me, and he nodded and took the paper.

"In a flash, he handed me a picture of not one, but two horses.

"And to my amazement, they were recognizable.

"When I stood before the audience, I announced proudly that I was going to talk to them about success. I asked, 'How many of you could draw me a picture of a horse?' There was only one small hand that went up, as everyone looked around, puzzled by the unexpected question.

"I bowed slightly in Josh's direction and said, 'Thank you, Josh, I hope you won't ever outgrow the ability to be

successful at whatever you are asked to do.'

"Then I explained to the perplexed crowd that most of us know how to be successful when we're very young because we believe we can do anything. It's only as we grow older and become conditioned by our environment and the people around us that we begin to doubt our ability. I held up Josh's picture and showed them that, not only did he do what I asked him to do—he did twice as much."

Jimmy Dick and little Josh have a lot in common. I've always believed that successful people are those who do what unsuccessful people refuse to do. No one has taught Josh that there is a limit to what he can achieve, and no one has convinced Jimmy Dick!

real-life stories

Bud Stoner

Bud Stoner is proof-positive that network marketing has come of age in corporate America. A successful corporate businessman who retired at 45, Bud is back in business with a capital "B."

"I don't even call it multilevel or networking," Bud says pointedly. "We are a DIRECT marketing company. I run my telecommunications business closer to a 'traditional' business than anyone else."

That's not surprising given the success Bud had in 'traditional' business. When Bud's employer, Builder Marts of America, had a $1 million phone bill one month, they decided to route their own calls to save money. They had excess capacity, which they sold to local businesses in Greenville, South Carolina. This sideline became so lucrative that Bud was recruited to work in the phone business full-time.

"Three vice-presidents from Builder Marts formed Tel Man Inc., which eventually went public and became

Southern Net, then Telecom USA. In June of 1990, MCI bought it for $1.2 billion."

After spending a few years racing Porches and scuba diving around the world, Bud is building another business in network marketing. Why network marketing?

"At first I wouldn't get involved. I figured I knew all there was to know about the telephone business and I saw no fit for network marketing in the phone business. Boy, was I wrong!"

Bud has specifically targeted successful professionals for his downlines.

"I talk to surgeons, judges, attorneys. I'm building my business on executive entrepreneurs who see the fabulous cash flow potential of residual income. That's the key. For many of these professionals, no matter how highly paid they are, they are still punching a clock. They only get paid if they come in.

"Then I show up and tell them about a cash flow instrument that will allow them to slow down and have a soft landing in the future so that when they retire, they will have a substantial income. I tell them to think of it as a 401(k) or retirement program for themselves.

"I've had 22 people leave full-time careers to go into network marketing full-time."

How do professionals respond to Bud's invitation to join a network marketing business?

"They respond very well...once they see the numbers. Many very successful people run their network marketing business on emotion. We run ours on numbers and cash flow. These people respond to that.

"Of course, there are some 'unbelievers' out there who can't believe what's happening.

"Sometimes they're just too proud to admit that this is an opportunity. And some people refuse because they had a bad experience with network marketing in the past. I understand that feeling, but people need to realize we've reached the third generation of the network marketing industry.

"Refusing to get aboard with network marketing today is like getting on a hot air balloon then refusing to fly a 747 years later."

After years of success, both in traditional and (to use Bud's term) "direct" marketing, Bud offers some basic advice:

"Never ever quit. In this business, you are woefully underpaid at the beginning and grossly overpaid when it matures. It's like pushing on a railroad car. It's very difficult getting it moving. But stay with it and your organization will get bigger than you are.

"And remember, this is a business. Every business needs emotion and enthusiasm, but you also need to focus on the bottom line, particularly when talking to successful business people.

"Show them the numbers, let them see the opportunity, then stand back. For people who truly understand business, this is an opportunity they can't afford to miss."

chapter nine

Attitude is everything!

(How I made myself a winner.)

As I've said, in network marketing more than any other business, you cannot be successful without a positive attitude. You can either be a winner or a whiner, but you cannot be both. But isn't it wonderful to know that no matter what your attitude may be right now, you have the power to change it?

You've heard the expression, "He's got an attitude!" This usually indicates a bad attitude, but it doesn't have to. Our church did a musical called "We've Got an Attitude!" that was positive and uplifting. We ALL have an attitude, just like we all are examples—either good or bad! And, more importantly, we each have a choice about this attitude. But we don't make a choice just once and for all. We make a choice for each individual thought we have. If you could weigh your thoughts on a scale, which side would be heavier, the positive or the negative? Whichever side wins determines your attitude!

All my life, I had operated on the precept that thoughts came from my mind, and there was very little I could do to control or change them. I was wrong! I have everything to do with it. I put them in—every single one of them.

When I say someone makes me angry—that's not true! No one

can make me angry except myself. We have been conditioned to believe that emotions and thoughts are caused by others, or by outside forces. When someone does something I don't like, I have a choice! I can choose to be upset, or I can choose not to be upset. I can dislike what someone does without letting myself become angry about it. When I fully understood the impact making choices has on my life, it was exhilarating! I had the power to make my emotional life exactly what I wanted it to be.

All negative emotion was unnecessary, wasted emotion! Of course, I discovered that understanding this concept is much easier than actually applying it on a regular basis. But the more I practiced, the better I got.

I have become especially good at controlling depression. I once lived with the mistaken belief that occasional bouts of depression were unavoidable. Now I can see how effective it is to refuse to tell yourself that you are depressed. If you determine to remain positive, it becomes almost impossible to become depressed. There may be exceptions for people with clinical, or medically diagnosed, depression. But for most of us, we must allow ourselves to sink into depression. It doesn't happen automatically. What a revelation!

Unfortunately, most of us are programmed early on to embrace the negative. It is splashed across the front pages of our newspapers, it pours off the screens of our televisions, it saturates the lyrics of popular music. We must learn to "re-program" ourselves, to find opportunities to put positive ideas into our minds and take out the negative.

Overcoming the #1 Dream Killer

The #1 Dream Killer is a negative attitude. As I mentioned, negativity fills the media. Starting the morning with the doom and gloom of your local newspaper is the worst way to develop a positive outlook. If you're one of those people (like my husband Jim) who cannot make it through the day without the paper or the local TV news, try to get your news late in the afternoon so it won't color your entire day gray. Leave your home or begin your work at home (if you're lucky enough to work at home) with a positive expectation. Do some exercise, take your vitamins, get the oxygen flowing with some simple deep breathing exercises and listen to a motivational tape as you drive. You'll be ready to conquer the world!

But most importantly, program a positive thought into your neutral thought time. I can't emphasize this point strongly enough! We all spend a surprising amount of time "between thoughts," when some idle little thought will jump into your head if you don't put your own selection there. This time will reinforce whatever slant you choose to place on your mental journey each day. If you let your mind select for you, it will probably go to your weakest, most insecure point and reinforce a negative suggestion.

For instance, if you have a weight problem that makes you feel self-conscious and awkward, you may be telling yourself all day long "I'm so fat!" or "I hate myself!" or "I look like a pig!" and you probably don't even realize it! But not all overweight people are insecure; some have chosen to accept themselves as they are. This acceptance keeps these hurtful negative thoughts at bay, and it keeps them upbeat and motivated all day long.

In order to change your attitude you must insert a positive thought to replace every negative one you take out. Every time you find yourself thinking "can't," substitute "can." Whenever the word "won't" comes to mind, try "will." I promise you'll be amazed at the results. As Henry Ford said, "If you think you can't or you think you can, you're right."

You don't even have to believe it at first—just *think* it! If you repeat the thought often enough, your subconscious will begin to accept it as true. You see, the #1 Dream Killer isn't your ability—it's your attitude. You aren't born with a negative attitude, and you certainly don't have to keep it. The choice is yours!

Developing the #1 Dream Maker

If the #1 Dream Killer is a negative attitude, then it seems logical to assume the #1 Dream Maker is a positive attitude. Right—well, almost, but not quite! A positive attitude is one of the necessary components, but it's not the essential one. A person can have a positive attitude but have a difficult time expressing it to others. Enthusiasm is the magic ingredient that makes those dreams come true.

The word "enthusiasm" comes from a Greek phrase meaning "God within." To me, this means the purest part of us—our God-like attributes—shine through when we express genuine enthusiasm. But how do we develop this magic? In my training class, I teach that the last four letters of "enthus-IASM" stand for "I-Am-Sold-Myself." Translated into network marketing, this means that a personal knowledge or satisfactory experience with the product or service sold can generate much-needed energy and enthusiasm.

I admit I've seen some people display great enthusiasm over items they probably aren't completely sold on. The enthusiasm may stem from the income generated by their performance. For example, in a TV advertisement you often see actors who seem very "enthusiastic" about shampoo, toothpaste and dog food. This may be a result of personal experience, or it may be related to the large sums of money they get to do the commercials.

You might say they are just acting. You would be exactly right. But if they act enthusiastic long enough, they will begin to feel it and implant that enthusiasm in their subconscious until it becomes real on the inside. The subconscious mind sends a signal to the physical body, and before you know it, the adrenaline is flowing and the excitement is genuine.

The power of Visualization

Visualization can play a major role in generating enthusiasm from within. Some view visualization as hokey and, to some, it probably is. But believe me, it works! We all visualize, but most people don't realize they are doing it.

I don't believe it works that way at all. I believe burning desires are ignited from the outside by our conscious mind. I honestly believe we can create a burning desire for anything we so choose. All of us wish for things, but we don't get them because we lack the courage to pursue them. They aren't really burning desires at all, just puffs of daydreams that float across our minds. We just think about them occasionally, half-heartedly, almost as if we're afraid to allow ourselves to get our hopes up.

How Visualization worked for me

About a year ago, we were living in a nice little house on a beautiful lake. I particularly loved the view—lots of water overlooking a peninsula densely covered with spectacular tall, green pine trees. The house was comfortable all week, but it seemed to suddenly shrink on weekends when our four grown sons, often accompanied by friends, wives and/or pets, arrived to spend a day with us.

We were always thrilled to have them, but every Saturday morning, our 15-year-old son (the only one still living at home) and several of his buddies ended up in sleeping bags on the living room floor. We had to step over them to get to the kitchen. Needless to say, he was not thrilled about it. I started thinking about perhaps adding a few rooms, but I concluded that it would be less expensive to build a new house. My husband, who was not at all interested in making any radical changes, regularly reminded me of the magnificent view from the entire rear of our home. I had to admit he was right.

While this discussion was going on, Jim and I were also suffering through months of construction noise as a big, Victorian home was going up on the point of our cul-de-sac, one house down from us. Driving up our street, this beautiful new home seemed to rise out of the lake like a mighty castle. I must admit I began to covet that house.

The new neighbors who built it were nice, so I didn't go so far as to wish they would have to put it on the market, but, ironically enough, that's exactly what happened. The owner was transferred to Ohio, and the house was listed for sale.

That evening, I asked Jim if he had heard the news, and he looked at me and shook his head. "Don't even think about trying to buy it," he said firmly. "We couldn't even qualify for a loan that big. I'm a state employee, and you're in network marketing."

"Well, they take cash, don't they?" I asked, trying not to laugh. "I'll just have to work real hard and see what I can come up with."

He laughed, too, and said, "Right! You do that, but don't get your hopes up. The chances of getting that place are slim to none!"

"We'll see!" I countered, grinning an evil little grin. "I can already see myself..." I began before he interrupted, "Please don't start that visualizing stuff. It just isn't practical for us."

I dropped the subject, but I had no intention of forgetting it. I had already decided to make this a "burning desire." I walked out the back door and headed for the castle. It was all locked up, but I could see most of the first floor through the windows along the wrap-around porch. The den had a big fireplace that was visible from the cooking island in the warm and inviting kitchen.

I pictured myself fixing meals while I watched my family in front of a hot, crackling fire. I heard music coming from the "Surround Sound" stereo system. "Eye of the Tiger" was playing. That song from "Rocky" always motivates me. I could feel the excitement building. I smelled the steaks on the gas grill, and I could hear them sizzle. I was getting hungry just standing there.

Then I turned and looked out over the 270 feet of deep water, and marveled at the breath-taking view. It was almost sunset, and the sky was streaked with gold and orange; the water looked dark blue, and there were geese flying in formation across the shaded sky. And most importantly, there was not a human being in sight! Not a marina, not a boat, just a huge, beautiful lake.

I knew at that moment that I was going to enjoy this view for a long, long time. I locked the pictures in my mind, then hurried home to finish cooking supper. All evening, I reinforced every detail in my mind, using as many of my senses as possible. I made plans to return the next day at the same time to touch the green grass, and dip my hands into the cold water from the dock in the backyard. I was making that place a part of me.

Somehow we would live there. I truly expected that to happen. All I had to do now was figure out how. I took the house with me everywhere I went for the next few days. I thought about it whenever my mind was in idle, and the more I thought about it, the harder I worked at my business. The burning desire was igniting a flame beneath my ambition. I kept telling my subconscious mind that something fabulous was going to happen to make my goal a reality! And guess what? My subconscious mind began to believe what my conscious mind was relaying. I began to think of ways to make this dream come true.

First, as always, I prayed for God's divine guidance. Then, I told the listing Realtor (who happened to be a good friend of mine) that we loved the house but couldn't afford it. A short time later he called Jim and told him that he ought to make an offer. My husband just laughed and said it would be embarrassingly low. "I'll probably just make them angry," he told the Realtor.

Finally, after a great deal of haggling back and forth, Jim made a pitifully low offer. I had agreed to make the offer, with the attitude that we had nothing to lose. However, Jim hadn't mentioned that it was one of those "no contingency" offers that, once accepted, had to be paid by a certain date. It didn't matter if you sold your own house or if had been approved for the loan. Once accepted, you had 30 days to write the check.

You guessed it: They accepted our offer

We had one month to get the money, we hadn't even put our house on the market, and we had no visible way to get the cash we needed. But for some reason, I wasn't even worried. I was already mentally living in that house and I was certain it would all come out fine. I fully expected to get that house, and I truly believe you get what you expect. Besides, I don't just *believe* in miracles, I *depend* on them. I also depend on doing my share to make them happen, so I laid out the necessary steps to make our dream house a reality.

I was working with 10 representatives in my downline. I knew I would soon be receiving almost $4,000 for bringing them in and helping them sign up their first few customers. I also knew I would be getting $165 for every new representative they signed up. Each of my representatives needed 10 reps in their downline to reach the first promotion, so one of my goals was to motivate my 10 reps to get to this promotion in the next 30 days. That would give me almost $20,000.

Because I was a trainer for my company as well as a representative, I knew I could also make another $20,000 training new representatives. By adding this income to the bonuses and overrides I would be earning, as well as the large amount of income I received monthly on the long distance usage of my telephone downline, would be just enough to get the house closed within our borrowing limit.

Just two weeks later, the same Realtor who told Jim to "make an offer," sold our small home to a minister and his wife for exactly what we needed to get out of it. The miracle came true. The closing went smoothly, and I began to walk the very floors and look out the very windows that I had dreamed of.

Some of our friends said we were so lucky—others thought the hard work had paid off. But I knew it was more than luck or work—it was that "burning desire" created through visualization. It works every time!

real-life stories

Henry Heath

Ask Reverend Henry Heath. He calls it a miracle.

"I have always believed in miracles. I think that they happen in unpredictable and unexpected ways. Such has been the case for me."

Thus began my fascinating conversation with Reverend Henry Heath and his beautiful wife, Gladys, two of the most precious people I've met in network marketing.

After 43 years of marriage, Henry and Gladys have found a way they can earn retirement income, help friends and neighbors start their own businesses and, perhaps best of all, work together.

Henry and Gladys have been a team since his college days.

"When Henry and I fell in love he wasn't even thinking of entering the ministry," Gladys told me. "Henry was called up to Korea, and while he was away, he wrote me and told me he was going to enter the ministry when he returned."

She paused and smiled. "I thought a long time before I answered that letter. When he came back, we were married and he went to Duke University to get his Divinity degree."

Thus began a long and fruitful partnership. Henry and Gladys have three beautiful daughters, and literally thousands of spiritual "children" in churches across the southeast.

"Being a priest is a 24-hour-a-day job," Henry told me. "I told my parishioners to call me anytime, day or night, if I could help them in any way. And the calls came, too."

Both Henry and Gladys have business backgrounds separate from the ministry. Before becoming a priest, Henry had been a commissioned salesman for a pharmaceutical company.

Gladys has 12 years of experience as a Realtor.

"In twelve years, she never wrote a contract she didn't close," Henry bragged to me. But Gladys was quick to point out that real estate sales provides no residual income. "That's why network marketing is important to us."

I asked Henry and Gladys how they got started in network marketing so late in life.

"We were looking for a little business we could do together," said Gladys. "But we never found the right one, until we went to a meeting for our network marketing company."

That meeting almost didn't take place. Here's the story Henry told me :

"We had retired to Seabrook Island, near Charleston, SC, and Gladys had designed our home.

"A friend from Greenville called us one day and said: 'Henry, I'm starting a new business and I want to come down and show it to you.' 'I'm not interested in a new business', I told him.

" 'What kind is it?' He replied: 'Long distance phone service.' I said, 'Now I'm even LESS interested, but please come down and see Gladys' house.'

"Our friend came down and encouraged us to go to a presentation. I asked Gladys if she wanted to go. She said no, but added, 'If you go, I'll go.' So we went, but very reluctantly.

"And we signed up the very first night," Henry concluded with a laugh.

What drew a minister, with years of theological training

and service, to network marketing?

"First of all, to be a priest, you must care deeply about people. And network marketing is about the people, not the product. I also enjoy teaching and counseling. I taught college during my days in the ministry, and other ministers often called on me to counsel others.

"Sharing network marketing with others often involves teaching them about the opportunity and helping them decide if it's right for them."

Gladys pointed out another attraction of network marketing.

"At that first meeting, Henry said what we need is a little business we can work together, even though we're not business people. And he was right. But this is a little business we can work together and *not* be business people. We saw that potential," Gladys said.

So they began their business, working part-time, in October of 1994. They had steady success until March of 1995 when Henry suffered a massive stroke, completely paralyzing his right side. Henry spent three months in an Atlanta hospital and another three months at home in bed.

"There was a time when we didn't know if I would ever recover," Henry told me. "I told my wife then, 'Don't feel sorry for me. I have a wonderful wife, three beautiful daughters and seven precious grandchildren. And besides, after all the years I spent in a pulpit, not even a stroke can keep me from talking!'

"But like I said, I believe in miracles." And miraculously, Henry completely recovered from his stroke and has returned to his network marketing business.

"Financially, we have modest goals. This is a part-time business that blesses us in many ways. Obviously, there is motivation to make money, but I think the idea they drum into you is that this business is like a family, from the highest level to the newest representatives.

"If we never make another penny, we've already changed some lives. And I hope to change a few more."

real-life stories

Kurt Berger

Kurt Berger says, "When a person believes in something, when they're committed and focused, get out of the way!" And he should know.

After only eight months of part-time work in network marketing he was able to leave his full-time job with the Internal Revenue Service.

"That's what makes network marketing so terrific," says Kurt. "This isn't about money, it's about freedom. I was 27 years old, looking at another 30 years of service, then collecting a pension and retiring. I wanted more, but that's all my IRS job could offer."

Kurt grew up as a Navy brat, spending time in Italy, Guam and New Orleans before settling in Charleston, South Carolina. "My dad said I could go to any college I wanted, but the only one he would *pay* for was The Citadel."

After graduation, Kurt eventually went to the IRS.

Nobody likes paying taxes,

especially people who have gotten behind and are getting visits from the IRS. "It was a tough job,"says Kurt. "It has to be done, because it's not fair for one business to pay while the one across the street refuses to pay its fair share. At the same time, I saw a lot of people in pain. One man even sat a gun on his desk and told me he was going to commit suicide. That is true desperation."

This is a sad truth, one that Kurt saw demonstrated every day. Many of us are trapped in jobs or businesses with relatively little hope for rapid income growth. If we get behind, it is almost impossible to catch up.

But with network marketing, the income potential is unlimited. There is no guarantee of great wealth, but there is always the possibility. You have the hope, the opportunity and the potential to achieve great wealth and true financial freedom.

"When I was approached about this telecommunications company, I had no interest in network marketing at all," says Kurt. "But Billy Hankinson, a good friend of mine whom I really trusted, told me I should check it out.

" 'I know all about these deals,' I told him. 'They promise the world and never deliver.'

" 'You remember the boy who cried wolf?' he asked. 'Well, this time there really *is* a wolf.'

"So I went to a presentation by Billy's mother, Betty Miles, and she made some cracks about the IRS," laughs Kurt. "After the meeting I gave her a business card and said, 'I hope you enjoy your audit.' "

Kurt came back to three or four meetings without signing up. "I was auditing the program, analyzing the business, trying to find the catch. Billy's wife was telling him, 'Oh, Kurt's never going to sign up, quit calling him.'

"But finally my wife and I sat down and decided we would give it a year. Just one year. If we weren't making a significant income from network marketing by then, we would get out. Amazingly, in less than half that time I was making more from the new business than from my so-called 'real job.' "

Kurt was only networking part-time, and he certainly could have stayed with the IRS. That's what network marketers mean by freedom—having the choice to work as much, or as little, as you want.

"When I handed in my resignation and quit the IRS for a part-time job, people really noticed. Why, in our first meeting, four out of the five people there signed up! And the one guy who didn't join the program came back a few months later and asked how I was doing. I showed him some of my checks and my letter of resignation, and he said: 'I must have missed something, can you show me again?' Today, he's a rep."

That's one of Kurt's secrets to success: Persistence. "When people told me they weren't interested in network marketing, I asked them: 'Do you want me to come back when I'm making $2,000 a month? OK, how about $5,000?' I have already gone back to all these people, and many of them have signed up with me.

"A few even told me to come back when I hit $10,000 a month. I hope to be visiting them in the near future," Kurt told me with a smile.

Kurt's experience in the IRS has given him a heartfelt desire, an almost evangelistic fire, to reach people with this opportunity. "I've gone back to some of the people I had to visit as a collector for the IRS, so I could show them a way out, a way they can have hope, do better, be free of the fear I saw when I first visited them. This is what makes network marketing worthwhile, helping yourself while you're helping others."

"It's about hope, about being positive," concludes Kurt. "I always tell people to check their blood type. If it's not 'Be Positive,' then get a transfusion."

real-life stories

Diane Chapman

The eighth of nine children born on a farm in the rural south, Diane Chapman has risen to become one of the most successful network marketers I've ever met, with an income in excess of $50,000 a month.

She's had two successful network marketing careers, the first as a financial planner with A.L. Williams (now PrimAmerica), and currently with a national telecommunications company.

Whatever the program, the source of Diane's success is the same: A vibrant personality, a positive enthusiastic attitude, and a passion for helping other people succeed.

"I got involved with A.L. Williams because I was interested in what they did for people. My parents passed away while I was in college, and they didn't really have adequate insurance. I was a student with no money, and that was an additional financial burden.

"As a rep for A.L. Williams, I was able to educate people, to help them protect their families and prepare for their futures. My job wasn't sales, it was teaching—teaching people how to take care of their finances and their families. And because it was network marketing, I was also building a business of my very own.

"I'm an enthusiastic person, but I'm not a high-pressure seller. The company taught us a sales approach which emphasized education, not pressure. We would teach people about their financial needs, then come back with a recommendation. I'm proud of the fact that, not only did I have many customers, but I delivered on claims that made a significant impact on their lives."

Diane got involved in network marketing through a friend. At first, she was skeptical.

"What got me over my distaste for network marketing was the potential for unlimited income, for finally being in charge of my own life. I had a college degree, I had a job, but I didn't have hope that I would ever achieve my life's goals. Network marketing makes it possible. All you need is a desire and a dream.

"For ordinary people with ordinary backgrounds and limited capital, network marketing is the way to go. Your success isn't based on your abilities or assets alone. Instead, you can join people with like desires and connect for a common goal. Together, each one can achieve more.

"In network marketing you have to rely on others, and you know they are relying on you. It's surprising how often people will go the extra mile for a friend before they will do it for themselves. Many times I've come home tired, not very motivated, and then had someone in my downline call me asking me to do a presentation, to help them get to the next level. Now, if it were a presentation for my customers, for myself, I might put it off or procrastinate. But because I know someone else is counting on me, I do a little more.

"And let me tell you, that's the difference between winners and losers. Winners and losers do the same things, but the winners do what they do with enthusiasm and a little bit more."

So what does Diane do to achieve her amazing success in network marketing?

"Find the right people. If you're a good listener, if you can figure out what makes people tick and what they really want out of life, you can motivate them to get involved. It's all about people. You know what drives people away from network marketing? The people in it. But do you know what gets people involved in network marketing? The people in it. It's all about finding the right people.

"Also, you have to find the right program. It may sound cliche, but people don't care how much you know until they know how much you care. You've got to care about the people, but you also need to be excited about your company, about the opportunity.

"No company can promise that you'll see results, but they should promise that you'll see the opportunity.

"Once you've picked a company, look at the people you'll be working with, the people in your upline. You want to be part of a dynamic, excited organization. And the ingredient that separates a fired-up, pumped-up organization from a poor, dying one is enthusiastic leadership. That is the key.

"Organizations need three things: resources, communication and leadership. Just as sure as a body lives, it must exhale and inhale. The company can provide the resources and a communications device, but only the people in your upline can provide the enthusiastic leadership. Remember: the speed of the leader determines the speed of the pack.

"Finally, you've got to constantly be looking for prospects. You've got to keep looking for *them* because you never know who is looking for *you*.

"I often sign people up on airplanes. I always sit next to people on airplanes, even if I have to get up and change seats. I have a small flip chart that I sit out on the fold-down tray, and I act like I'm practicing my presentation. I whisper to myself phrases like 'unlimited income,' and 'financial freedom.' Without fail, the person next to me will ask what I'm doing.

" 'Oh, am I disturbing you? I'm so sorry,' I tell them.

" 'No, that's OK,' they reply. 'What is that company? Can you tell me about it?'

"I smile and say 'Well, if you're sure I'm not disturbing you...' "

Diane has one last message for anyone who has tried a network or multi-level program in the past:

"I've been involved in this a long time, and I'm familiar with many different programs. I know a lot of people who have succeeded and a lot who have failed. But I also know that the time has come, that for the average man or woman, network marketing is the most tremendous opportunity available.

"With my network marketing experience, sometimes I feel like the dove who flew out of Noah's Ark to test the land. Now, I've returned with an olive branch, a message of hope. I can tell you that, hallelujah, the land is dry."

Diane understands how to make dreams come alive...her enthusiasm for this business is doing it for many, many others.

chapter ten

My dream is for everyone

My dream for you and everyone who reads this book is simple. I hope you find the right vehicle to enable you to achieve your American Dream.

If you're wondering if network marketing could possibly be for you, ask yourself a few simple questions:

1) If you had it to do over again, would you do the same type of work or have the same kind of business you do now?

2) Is your job or business providing enough income to meet the needs and wants of you and your family without your getting heavily into debt?

3) Do you have time to enjoy your life—do you have the freedom to do the things you want to do when you want to do them?

If you can answer "yes"to all three questions, you are a fortunate person, and I would recommend that you stay focused. Of course, it couldn't hurt to have your spouse check out network marketing.

If you can answer "yes" to the first two questions but "no" to the third, you might want to consider trying network marketing on a part-time basis until your income from the new company equals the income from your regular business. Then you would have a choice, a new level of personal freedom. I believe you would find network marketing is even more enjoyable than your other work because of the personal satisfaction from helping people change their lives for the better.

If you can answer "yes" to the first and third questions—that is, you love your work and have plenty of time, but you just can't make ends meet—you definitely need to consider network marketing. In fact, if you continue where you are, you probably won't be able to answer "yes" to the third one very long because you'll need to find a second or third job as you get farther and farther behind.

If you answer "yes" to the second and third questions, you are a candidate because no amount of money or free time is worth being unhappy or dissatisfied with your job or business.

If you still are wondering if network marketing is for you, see if these suggestions help you decide:

If you're a college student, going into your final year of college or maybe getting ready for that big graduation day, remember what you read in this book. Today, you might be filled with excitement and hope, perhaps just a little bit anxious and apprehensive because you took the first job you were offered (many of your classmates may have had no offers at all!).

Now is the time to start working on that positive attitude right away. Never forget that you get what you expect, and that you are in control of what goes into your mind. Dr. Norman Vincent Peale once said, "Change your thoughts, and you change your world." Do you believe it? If you don't, start thinking that you do. That's all it really takes. To be a positive person, all you have to do is think you are and tell yourself you are until you begin to believe it. Isn't that awesome power?

If you love your new job, that's great, but keep a positive outlook on life and remember that you have options. If you don't like your current job, don't just drift from one dissatisfying job to another—take a look at network marketing. You may never have to work for anyone else again, and there's no limit on the amount of income you could earn.

And how blessed you are to have your whole life before you to maximize your potential. If I weren't having so much fun, I might envy you myself!

If you are long past those college days, perhaps never had a chance to go, but you always dreamed of giving your kids a college education, what will you do when the big corporation you've worked for the last 20 years decides to do a little downsizing? What happens when you're one of the first to go. So now what do you do?

I'll tell you. Tell the kids to get a student loan—they'll qualify now that you're unemployed.

In fact, your college kid can check it out with you. Many college students are working with network marketing companies to help pay for their educations.

And then they'll have something exciting to do after graduation.

If you're one of the many people who have been forced to take early retirement, don't get down in the dumps. Congratulate yourself! This may be the most fortuitous event in your entire business career. Imagine being given an incentive bonus to go out into the world and make a fortune helping other people make theirs. What a wonderful way to spend your twilight years.

I have mentioned doctors, lawyers and politicians, but the most likely candidates for network marketing can often be found in sales. Successful salesmen are frustrated because the more they make in commissions, the more the large companies try to reduce the size of their territories, or lower the percentage of their commissions, or worse yet, yank them out of the field and put them in a low-paying management position.

Commissioned salesmen have an additional problem to worry about—interactive television and telephone are going to make it very difficult for them to earn a living when all the products they sell can be bought direct—and *without* a commission. Cars, houses, insurance policies and just about every other product on the market will be sold over the interactive telephone.

I've already seen ads on TV selling insurance policies direct, and houses are being purchased over the Internet, airline tickets, too. If you sell a commissioned product, you need to prepare to make some changes.

Attorneys have a problem, too—there are just too many of them. Also, they're limited by the number of hours they can dedicate to their profession. They never get paid vacations because the overhead doesn't go away when they do.

Lawyers also bear another burden: lack of credibility. That's really a shame, because most of them are hard-working, honest and dedicated to helping people, but a few rotten ones have tainted the image for everyone. (In the interest of fairness, I probably should remind you that Jim is an attorney).

The thought of tainted images brings me to another group who constantly face public scrutiny and criticism—politicians. Since I've had an inside glimpse of the political world, I can tell you that it's incredible what politicians face every day. I'll never understand how we have enough people to fill all the elected positions, and I truly believe this will become more and more difficult if the environment doesn't become less hostile.

I could go on and on about the types of people who are trying network marketing for the first time. They come from every walk of life, from every profession, and they have one very important concept in common—they still believe in the American Dream. This marketing concept, like franchising, has gone through a remarkable metamorphosis, but it has emerged as the most effective way to retain loyal customers. The stigma it once had is slowly fading as the income levels skyrocket. I predict that network marketing will create more millionaires in the next ten years that any other type of business. My dream is that every one of you will be one of them, but it will remain just that—a dream—unless you decide to make it a goal. The opportunity is there for every single one of you, and it won't go away if you miss it, it will just go to somebody else!

My dream for my family

The first week I was in the business, I rushed around to every member of my family—immediate, intermediate, and extended—and literally begged them to join me in this fascinating business. That was two and a half years ago, and I was raving about the information highway and the telecommunications revolution and all the incredible things that were going to take place once the utility monopolies were broken up. I told them about the interactive telephones that were coming and satellite cellular telephones that would do all sorts of tasks.

But you know what? They didn't really care about all that high tech information. They just got caught up in my excitement; they wanted to do it because I was doing it. My enthusiasm was as contagious as a virus and soon everyone was infected: aunts, uncles, cousins, nieces, nephews, second and third cousins, etc., etc.

It was fun for me to renew old relationships and help them build their business, but after a month or two, the novelty wore off and most of them returned to what they were doing before. The telecommunications company we had joined was new in our state and I didn't know enough about the business to give them a clear track to run on. In the end, most of them eventually lost interest.

My oldest son, Billy Hankinson, worked it harder than any of the others, but he had a new wife, Kerry, and they wanted to buy a house and start a family. After a short time, he went back to concentrating full-time on his regular job with a national office supply company.

But showing wisdom beyond his years, Billy reassessed his situation and drew some insightful conclusions. Here's what he told me when I asked him to describe what network marketing has meant to him and his family:

> I saw network marketing for the first time in October of 1993. My mother, Betty Miles, told me I needed to come hear about this great telecommunications business she had just gotten into. She told me the company was getting its customer base through network marketing. So, I went. I got excited and signed up that night, but when I got home my wife, Kerry, was not very excited. Both of our families were involved in the business, and she didn't want to just follow the crowd.
>
> I signed up a couple of representatives and a few customers, then decided maybe Kerry was right. I put the network marketing business on hold. At my "real job," I had been promoted to sales manager with an office equipment company just a few months earlier. My new position took a lot of time, and I felt like I should put my focus on this safe, secure opportunity (even though my pay plan had been reduced by over $10,000 per year). Kerry was selling insurance part time and was very successful, but she sometimes had to wake up at 3:30 and 4:00 in the morning to get to her appointments on time.
>
> In January of 1995, Kerry and I were blessed with a baby girl, Katelyn Brooke Hankinson.
>
> She changed everything! We wanted Kerry to be able to stay home with Brooke, so we started trying to find ways to accomplish that. We knew my mom was doing very well in the network marketing business, but one weekend when we went to visit her, we met another young couple with a new baby boy, (Scotty, Lori and Jake Salter). They were doing network marketing full-time! That was when we decided that we could do this.
>
> So, in March of 1995, we started working on our network marketing business with the modest goal of allow-

> ing Kerry to stay home with Brooke. After six months, our part-time business had replaced both of our incomes, so we decided to start putting a full-time effort into it. It has been the best personal and financial decision that we have ever made!
>
> Network marketing has given us the freedom to travel when we choose, get out of debt, make more money, work fewer hours and more importantly, spend time as a family. Most people will never know the freedom of being their own boss and making their own income.
>
> But more importantly, most people will spend more time at their "job" than they will spend watching their children grow up and holding their spouse. Now that I know what it is like to work for myself, I don't ever want to have to work for someone else again.

Network marketing is changing America! It's giving many young couples the opportunity to be financially independent, the wonderful opportunity to be whole families again. Billy and Kerry have more than doubled their combined incomes of a year ago, and although I'm thrilled with their financial success, I'm much more excited to know my precious little granddaughter isn't having to spend most of her waking hours in a day care center while her parents resent the missed moments with Brooke they can never recapture.

My second son, Clint Hankinson, graduated from Baylor University last May and is now the assistant youth minister at Fellowship Baptist Church in Columbia, South Carolina. It's a small church, and they couldn't afford to pay much, but Clint started working in this networking business while he was out in Texas, and he plans to use the income he earns to supplement his church income. Clint now has options because his part-time business is producing residual income that will continue to grow even when he is no longer working the business.

Some of the college students Clint recruited into this business have graduated and have taken new opportunities to their friends and families all over the country. We have made some very dear friends through this industry.

My youngest son, John Hankinson, is just 17 and a rising senior at Chapin High School, and he is excited about the possibility of never having to work for someone else in his entire lifetime. He plans to join our networking company as soon as he's 18 and he says he'll be a millionaire by the time he's 21. And you know what? I think he just might do it.

My husband, Jim, has two sons, Mel and Jeffrey Miles, and they're both excited about this business, too. Jeff is living in Puerto Rico, and since this telecommunications company hasn't expanded to that area yet, he is reluctantly having to wait. He has laid a lot of ground work, however, so I'm sure it won't take him long to sign up just about everyone there once it opens. Jeff is a natural salesman.

Mel, Jim's older son, had just launched a very successful career in the financial services industry when I found this business. He really loved what he was doing, so I didn't try to persuade him to try network marketing because I was so happy that he was enjoying his chosen field. I really didn't want him to get unfocused. He is an outstanding leader in his company and already in the top 1% of all income earners in the country.

Mel is also a very lucky man because his beautiful new wife, Shelley, has decided she wants to stay home when she has a baby. She's a school teacher, and she made a deal with Mel. If her income in the network marketing business equaled her teaching income by the end of the summer, she wouldn't go back in the fall. Now, they can begin to plan for their first child much earlier than they had thought.

That covers the immediate family, but this business doesn't stop there. Billy's wife, Kerry, has already recruited her father, Jerry Dupuy, who likes the telecommunications business so much he's just sold his successful building business to do this full-time. Kerry also signed up her mother and stepfather, Virginia and Rick Philbeck. Virginia owns her own business and her husband is an eye doctor. Who knows, if things continue to

My Family

(back) Billy, Clint, John, (front) Kerry, Betty and Brooke

Shelley

go well, they may be joining us full-time, too.

Mel's wife, Shelley, has been busy bringing in her family as well. Her parents, Bunny and Don Hagenlocher (they're the fine photographers who did the cover photo) are excited about this business because, even though they like the photography industry, their business is very labor intensive. Like all small business owners, they only get paid for the hours they work, and they never get a paid vacation. Shelley is also recruiting her two sisters, Sherri Hagenlocher and Stacy Leventis.

Now, since I'm the oldest of five, you can just imagine how many of my siblings I signed up.

My sister, Sharon Rexford, tried it for a little while, but she just wears too many hats to find time for even a part-time business. She's a nurse, a social worker, a foster mom (several times over), a political candidate, a Christian Coalition member, a political activist and a few other things I can't think of right now. My baby sister, Maria York, has tried it twice, but she's busy helping her hubby, Bill, get his new consulting firm up and running, and she's also trying to keep up with their three gorgeous daughters who play all sorts of sports, play in the band, perform in plays and get invited to the Governor's Mansion in Atlanta and the White House in Washington. But I haven't given up on either of them, yet. They can't resist forever. And besides, those girls will be old enough soon.

My third sister, Fran McSwain, lives in Shelby, North Carolina, and she's been in since the beginning. She's the sister I mention in my business presentations, the one who's too shy to stand up in front of a large group. Her 14-year-old son, Walter, came to visit me last summer and I took him all over North Carolina while I was doing meetings. By the time he got home, he had memorized the presentation chart. Now, all my sister has to do is invite a few friends over and Walter can do the business presentation for her.

My brother, John Fili, was the one I thought would enjoy this business most because he had been in sales for years, but he was the last one to come in. In fact, he's just beginning. One important aspect about network marketing is timing. If a person is not ready to make a commitment, do not push. They'll do the business when it's right for them. Besides, his son Michael will be old enough to join us in a few years, and they can work together.

I saved the best for last. When I began this business three years ago, I was told to get my mother as a telephone customer rather than as a marketer. The trainer said, "Your mother will help you out." Well, he didn't know what a spunky mother I have. When I asked her to try this company's long distance service, she listened for a few minutes, then said, "Who do you think taught you how to sell? I want to be a marketer!" She was already in her seventies, even though she looks and acts more like fifty, and I was so proud of her attitude.

She was right, too. She did instill self-confidence in me, by focusing on and praising my positive attributes and accomplishments. She told me I could do anything that I wanted to do, and she made me believe it. She gave that wonderful gift to all her children. After every disappointment in our personal or professional lives, Mother has been there for us. She is truly a remarkable woman.

I'm looking forward to the next few years in the telecommunications industry. It's growing and changing so fast. I love this business. It's been a blessing for our family in many ways.

My dream for you and for everyone who reads this book is very simple. I hope you find the right vehicle to enable you to achieve your American Dream. For me that vehicle was network marketing, and I've shared with you as much as I can about this marketing concept.

There's much more, of course, but the rest is something you have to experience for yourself.

I hope I've at least convinced you that it's possible for you to change your life, too. You may or may not decide to make that stretch—to reach for the freedom that's within your grasp—but I wanted to share with you some of the possibilities. The rest is up to you!

Glossary

Audio presentation – Many companies have audio tapes available to help marketers recruit new reps. The actual business presentation is put on an audio cassette tape that is convenient to listen to in the car. Some companies put their training program on audio tape and include it in the initial supply kit for new reps. Most network marketing companies also offer audio tapes with testimonials by their leading producers. These tapes are also good for mailing to prospects in other cities and states.

Business Presentation (BP) – A presentation of information about the financial opportunity being offered by a particular company, as well as specific information about the company and its products or services. Some companies have company presenters who do regularly scheduled meetings based on a script the company has approved. Most companies have video and/or audio tapes with the standard, approved BP which can be purchased from the home office. Some companies allow individual representatives to make business presentations, but require these individuals to follow the approved script in an effort to maintain the integrity of the company.

Circle of Influence – Each individual has a group of close friends and family over which he has some influence and, therefore, this group is more likely to be receptive as a prospect for the representative. If the rep approaches more receptive individuals in the early stages of their business, they will have the opportunity to gain knowledge and experience before they attempt to recruit people who are outside this circle.

Commission – The percentage of the service fee that you are paid for selling a service. When selling a product, the commission is the difference between the wholesale price and the retail price.

Distributor – A person who signs an agreement with a multi-level marketing company to offer the company's product or products to the general public. The distributor is recruited by a sponsor who helps the distributor duplicate the business procedures of the sponsor. Also called a representative, an independent representative, or a sales representative.

Downline – A term used in network marketing to describe the individuals recruited by the representative as well as those recruited by the recruits. For example, A signs up B and C. B signs up D, E and F. C signs up G, H and I. B through I would all be considered A's downline.

Headhunting fees – Used by illegal pyramid schemes to pay people in the business for recruiting new people into the business. New people are charged an entry fee for joining the business. This money goes to the people who recruited them.

Information or Technology Revolution – A descriptive term for the high-tech period of time from the 1970's into the 21st century, when very creative individuals, such as Bill Gates and Paul Allen began to develop the computer technology which will take all of us into a new futuristic world of computerized technology that will greatly enhance the quality of life for most people.

Information Highway – Name sometimes used to describe the conveyor belt that will deliver a vast number of products and services during the Information or Technology Revolution.

Inventory loading – Method used by companies which requires new distributors to purchase large amounts of nonreturnable merchandise. Part of the company's proceeds from each distributor's order then goes to that person's sponsor.

Leadership Bonus – This is a bonus that is paid to network marketers for helping the people they sponsor move up to a higher level in the organization or reach some requirement the organization requires.

Multi-level marketing (MLM) – A method of distributing goods and services through word-of-mouth advertising rather that by the use of conventional advertising or retail outlets. This method of marketing is fast becoming the preferred way to accumulate loyal customers. Also, his represents another way of selling goods and services through a tiered structure of independent distributors.

Multiplier Effect – The ability to make money, not only from your own sales, but from the sales of the people you sign up in the organization and from the sales of the people they bring into the organization, etc.

Pyramid Schemes – (Also known as Ponzi Schemes after the man who originated the concept.) Newcomers to the group pay money to those who are already in the business, much like a chain letter. The new members must go out and find others in order to get paid. These pyramid schemes are illegal because the people who get in in the early stages of the business are usually the only ones who make money and the pyramid falls apart as it becomes more and more difficult to get people into the business.

Residual Income – A commission that is paid on a customers' repurchases or renewals of products or services. This is income that is earned even after you stop working.

Upline – In the definition for downline above, A through H would be I's upline.

Appendix A

Court cases and laws have primarily dealt with two issues surrounding multi-level marketing. First, is the plan an illegal pyramid or Ponzi scheme? And second, does the plan in any way involve securities laws (the laws involving stock sales)? The courts have provided clear answers to these two questions which allow legitimate, product-driven, multi-level marketing plans to flourish.

Courts of law have examined Ponzi schemes and have rendered several important decisions. Two important cases which outline the legal elements of a Ponzi scheme are *In Re Agricultural Research and Technology Group.*, 916 F.2d 528, and *In Re United Energy Corp.*, 922 F.2d 589.

Both cases make it clear that intentional fraud and the absence of a real product or service are needed in a true illegal Ponzi scheme.

In Re Agricultural Research ruled that a Ponzi scheme was an arrangement where an enterprise makes payments to investors from later investors instead of from the proceeds of an underlying business. The case held that it is a fraud to transfer the proceeds from new investors to original investors thereby giving the false impression that actual profits are being generated. And in

In Re United Energy Corp., it was similarly held that the illusion of profits created merely through new investors is per se a fraud which makes a pyramid illegal.

Because Ponzi schemes often resemble investments, it is important to examine the law of securities. The most common types of securities are stock. But there are other investments that are often securities. These include the sale of limited partnerships, bonds, and notes. It is possible that a multi-level marketing plan may be structured in such a way that participation becomes a security, though this is rare. If a multi-level marketing plan is structured so that it becomes a security, it triggers certain regulations and restrictions. As we shall see, however, most modern multi-level marketing plans do not constitute securities.

The most famous Supreme court case involving securities was handed down in 1946. *SEC v. W.J. Howey,* 328 U.S. 293 (1946), was a landmark decision which is still used by today's lawyers and Courts to determine if investments like multi-level marketing plans are securities.

The Court in *Howey* held that a security is a plan or transaction where a person (1) invests his money, (2) in a common enterprise and (3) is led to expect profits (4) solely from the efforts of others. Because most multi-level marketing plans generally require some degree of monetary payment to begin participation, some may be suspicious that these plans are actually securities. But anyone who has worked in a multi-level marketing plan knows that obtaining "proceeds" involves work—your own work.

Remember, a security involves proceeds obtained solely through the efforts of others. For example, a stockholder earns dividends solely through the efforts of others. A stockholder generally has no contact with the company employees and management who generate their dividends. The stockholder does not contact customers. The stockholder does not work on the assembly line. Instead, they usually watch the reports of their increasing or diminishing wealth from a distance.

On the other hand, most multi-level marketing plans require work in order to earn proceeds. Success or failure in a legitimate multi-level marketing business is directly tied to the efforts of the individual. A Federal Appeals Court defined "solely through the efforts of others" to exclude multi-level marketing plans in *Securities and Exchange Commission v. Glen Turner Enterprises,* 474 F.2d 476 (9th Cir. 1973). The Court ruled that to be a security, the efforts of a third party other than the investor are "the undeniably significant ones, those essential managerial efforts, which affect the failure or success of the enterprise." In most modern multi-level marketing plans, the efforts and hard work of the investors are the ones which make all the difference. If no products or services are sold, no money is made.

The more contacts made, the more money made. The more products or services sold, the greater the profits. This is what separates multi-level marketing plans from securities and the laws regulating them.

Some early scam artists used methods which resembled modern multi-level marketing. They relied on several layers of investor-victims to generate cash flow. Also, early chain letter scam artists used multiple layers of victims to obtain cash flow. Both scams involved outright, good old fashioned fraud. They had no products for sale. Unlike these scams, most modern multi-level marketing plans are truthful and rely on the sale of products. Yet past scam artists using schemes which share some characteristics of multi-level marketing plans have given modern legitimate plans a bad reputation. The famous Amway decision in 1979 once and for all legitimized multi-level marketing plans.

In Re Amway, 93 F.T.C. 618 (1979), marks perhaps the most significant legal decision for all those seeking the new American Dream in multi-level marketing. The Federal Trade Commission decided to examine the legality of the most famous multi-level marketing company, Amway. Ultimately, the Commission ruled that Amway was not an illegal pyramid plan.

The Commission held that the modern multi-level marketing plan considered by it, was legitimate. It ruled that several characteristics of this plan solved many of the problems associated with illegal pyramid schemes of the past. The first problem was that investors were often stuck with significant amounts of unsold inventory. They were forced to buy the inventory in order to participate in the plan. Amway solved this problem by promising to buy back any unsold inventory.

The second problem associated with pyramids had been that revenues were generated primarily through the recruitment of new members instead of the sale of products. Start-up fees for new members dominated the revenue streams of early multi-level marketing schemes. On the other hand, the Commission recognized that success in Amway depended first and foremost on the sale of a product. If you didn't sell, you didn't earn commissions.

Amway also had a relatively small fee participants paid in order to enter into the marketing mix. Past multi-level marketing scams had required initial investments of thousands of dollars.

And finally, the Commission recognized that Amway sellers sold to individuals in the retail market. Amway sellers went beyond the Amway family to distribute products at retail prices. This is an important distinction between Charles Ponzi and modern salespersons in that the modern multi-level marketing salesperson is selling a product, not a false dream. These products are being purchased in the retail marketplace. Whether it is skin care products, phone service or audio equipment, retail customers not associated directly with multi-level marketing companies are buying their products. The Commission recognized that multi-level marketing not only opened up a wide range of economic opportunity for sellers, but also represented the introduction of greater selection for the consumer.

The Federal Trade Commission made one final cautionary note. A multi-level marketing presentation may not exaggerate potential earnings.

In the *Amway* decision, the Federal Trade Commission unleashed the powerful new business tool of multi-level marketing. They at last erased any lingering doubts about the legitimacy of multi-level marketing. The American Dream was brought within reach of tens of thousands of Americans who could not afford vast sums of investment capital to start their own business. This decision made it possible for business people who did not wish to devote large sums of cash to risky and often ineffective advertising campaigns to introduce products to the consumer. If the endeavor was product-driven, did not require large start-up fees, sold to the retail consumer market, and did not misrepresent earning and potential income it was legal, according to the FTC.

Appendix of interviews

Michael Warshaw and Duncan Anderson
Success Magazine
230 Park Avenue
New York, NY 10169
(212) 551-9300

Mack Ballard
3031 Tomlinson Road
Milledgeville, GA 31061
(912) 453-0082

Kurt Berger
8305 Vestige Court
Charleston, SC 29418
(803) 760-0389

Diane Chapman
Florence, SC
(803) 665-0319

Bill and Kerry Hankinson
1941 Tison Lane
Mount Pleasant, SC 29464
(803) 971-0077

Jimmy & Cathy Dick
12 Broad Street
Box 1776
Sumter, SC 29151
(803) 561-1017

Mickey & Leslie Tumlin
2832 Acton Place
Birmingham, AL 35243
(803) 802-8600

John & Beth Craver
1492 Pine Island View
Mount Pleasant, SC 29464
(803) 881-5481

Dr. Gene Bass
510 Mockingbird Drive
Long Beach, MS 39560
(601) 436-5708

Bob Capes
6 Washington Street
Suite 400
Columbia, SC 29201
(803) 343-2700

Lee Simonson
504 Morgan Drive
Lewiston, NY 14092
(716) 754-8414

Bud Stoner
105 Kettering Court
Greenville, SC 29607
(864) 371-8992

Kathryn Inabinet Laney
2 Medina Court
Columbia, SC 29223
(803) 561-1013

Steve Hammond
3002 Bellmont Blvd.
Nashville, TN 37212
(615) 783-0274

Sue Turner
133 Shute Circle
Old Hickory, TN 37138
(615) 847-0990

John Jones
117 Decatur Street
Brooklyn, NY 11216
(718) 574-4110

Beth Hinson
42 Church Street
Summerton, SC 29148
(803) 485-8305

Lloyd & Peggy Morris
Box 27470
Austin, TX 78755
(800) 749-0616

Dr. Joe Rubino
140 Union Street
Suite 303
Lynn, MA 01901
(617) 592-4438

The Reverend
Henry & Gladys Heath
2896 Baywood Drive
Johns Island, SC 29455
(803) 768-0504

John Pershing Smith and Bonnie Zane Smith
3550 Centerville Highway
Lithonia, GA 30338
(770) 979-9658

Ray Faltinsky
333 Quarry Road
Milford, CT 06460
(203) 882-7250